Pandemic Surveillance

Pandemic Surveillance

David Lyon

polity

First published in 2022 by Polity Press

Polity Press
65 Bridge Street
Cambridge CB2 1UR, UK

Polity Press
101 Station Landing
Suite 300
Medford, MA 02155, USA

ISBN-13: 978-1-5095-5030-2
ISBN-13: 978-1-5095-5031-9 (pb)

A catalogue record for this book is available from the British Library.
Library of Congress Control Number: 2021940596

Typeset in 11 on 14pt Sabon
by Fakenham Prepress Solutions, Fakenham, Norfolk NR21 8NL
Printed and bound in Great Britain by CPI Group (UK) Ltd, Croydon

For further information on Polity, visit our website:
politybooks.com

In memory of Bob Pike, faithful colleague; Saudager Jagdev, friend; and Chris Osborne, brother-in-law. COVID claimed their lives.

Contents

Acknowledgments

Many thanks to the kind people who have made this somewhat ambitious task more manageable, and even, at times, enjoyable. Those generous and patient souls who read my work and commented, sharing their expertise in computing, communications, law, medicine, public health, sociology and life experience, are Samantha Buttemer, Juanne Clarke, Tommy Cooke, Rodrigo Firmino, Martin French, Griffin Lyon-Wicke, Neil McBride, Benjamin Muller, Midori Ogasawara, Teresa Scassa, Sachil Singh, Emily Smith, Valerie Steeves, plus three perceptive anonymous readers recruited by Polity. Those who patiently offered ideas, stories, references and guidance include Rafael Evangelista, Rui Hou, Reetika Khera, David Leslie, Liza Lin, Jay Meehan, Nurhak Polat, Vidya Subramanian and Elia Zureik. Those giving support and encouragement include Mary Savigar, my editor at Polity, who helped to ease my early doubts; Jennifer Whitaker, who made the index; Emily Smith, who, despite her own pandemic-prompted domestic disruptions, still stood

Acknowledgments

strong; Sylvia Andrychuk, go-to surveillance librarian at the Stauffer; and of course – now after 50 years by my side – Sue, whose partnership and love are unwavering.

1

Defining Moments

It all happened very quickly. After some mildly worrying small-print news in January 2020, about a new virus in a Wuhan sea-food market in China, by February, news that the "novel coronavirus" was spreading quickly around the world became headlines. There was the predictable scramble to stock up on toilet paper, and less predictable advice to sanitize groceries. In March, a steel fence was erected round the climbing frame and swing sets in our local park, making it look like a crime scene, and masks started to appear on the faces of passers-by in the street. Not long afterwards, smart-phones were sought for pandemic service and I also found myself being called up for conversations about the use of personal data for public health platforms, so that the pandemic's path could be followed, and future developments modeled and predicted.

In the same month, news media started commenting on the sudden burgeoning of surveillance. Its main feature at that time was the rollout of the first digital contact tracing systems, using smartphones to identify contacts who may have been exposed to the virus. By April, tech giants Google and Apple had joined forces to support Bluetooth-based apps, a signal that platforms and governments were collaborating in such surveillance. Cautions about "false positives" and the need for accompanying testing and treatment facilities, plus fears regarding privacy intrusion, discrimination and marginalization were downplayed by those confident in the capacities of the silver bullet.

Surveillance was also sought for documenting where people are, where they'd been and their health status; data-modeling to track the spread of COVID-19; as well as identifying people who, potentially, had been exposed to infected others. Warnings were issued that there may well be civil liberties consequences as everyday technologies used for commerce, communication and convenience were marshaled for keeping close tabs on everyone, in the name of controlling the contagion. What is built for today may be normalized, worried some, such that they would persist after the virus is contained.

Now, the idea of using surveillance to get to grips with an outbreak of disease has a long history. Some salute John Snow, a London doctor who tried to discover the cause of the 1854 cholera epidemic, as a pioneer data scientist. At that time, a 'miasma' theory reigned, suggesting that bad air was to blame. A few years before, Snow had a new hypothesis that the "blue death" could be caused by cesspools, lack of sanitation and contaminated water in poor neighborhoods.

Scorned at the time, when the cholera came, Snow knocked on doors, inquiring about the source of each family's drinking water. The collected data pointed to a specific pump on Broad Street, Soho. This was confirmed by Reverend Henry Whitehead, initially skeptical of the polluted water idea, who checked further to see who had and had not used that pump. The pair removed the handle, effectively shutting off the water supply, and the cholera cases quickly dwindled.[1] The conviction that such data collection from infected people could aid the task of getting a grip on the germ is basic to epidemiology, a key discipline in public health.

What is "pandemic surveillance?"

This book is about pandemic surveillance. So, what is meant by each of these terms, and the two together? As it happens, each part of the word-duo is hard to define and is understood differently by different experts. The first term is "pandemic," generally referring to the widespread incidence of disease affecting "all" (*pan*) "people" (*demos*) and in use – as "pandemick" – since the 1660s. The fourteenth-century Black Death killed more than 100 million people in Asia and Europe – estimates vary – and the misnamed "Spanish Flu" (it did not originate in Spain) of 1918–20 infected half a billion and killed tens of millions. With improved transportation by railways and steamships, and the movement of troops after the First World War, the flu spread over a wider world. The COVID-19 pandemic is often qualified by the word "global," signaling that,

3

with air transport, cruise ships and complex long-distance haulage, few around the globe are untouched.

But what makes COVID-19 or any other disease a "pandemic?" Is it, for example, its explosive transmissibility, or the severity of infection, or both, perhaps with other features as well? Medical experts disagree and debate this. After the outbreak of the H1N1 influenza virus in 2009, an article in the *Journal of Infectious Diseases* debated various options, concluding that "simply defining a pandemic as a large epidemic may make ultimate sense in terms of comprehensibility and consistency."[2] Yet the same article makes many points about how pandemics relate to other factors such as urban population size, modes and ease of transportation, the state of medical knowledge, the actions of public health officials and the role of disease in domesticated animals. These point clearly toward *social*, *technical*, *economic* and *political* aspects of pandemics.

Indeed, one factor that connects "pandemic" with "surveillance" is that pandemics, however widely distributed, are far from *evenly* distributed. Even a nuanced reading of the Greek word *demos* hints at this, suggesting a social division between elites and the "common people" or "the crowd." While in the early 2020s no one in the world is untouched by the pandemic, at least as a social condition, people are affected with differing degrees of severity, often relating to social class, gender, race and other decidedly social factors. This became more marked as surveillance "solutions" appeared.

So, what is meant by "surveillance?" According to the World Health Organization (WHO), surveillance in relation to public health is the "ongoing, systematic collection, analysis and interpretation of health-related data essential to the planning, implementation and evaluation of public health practice."[3] It is undertaken to inform disease prevention and control measures. Understood this way, it has clear human benefit and should thus be a priority among the available tools for confronting a pandemic, especially a global one. As we shall see, however, the WHO also notes the social and other dimensions of such surveillance, and warns that surveillance tools are *not* neutral and may be used in ways that challenge other priorities such as human rights and civil liberties.

More generally, we may think of surveillance as any purposeful, focused, systematic and routine observation and attention to personal details. Those "personal details" are sought, today, in digital data, made available in multiple formats that can snowball in some contexts. For instance, the data for contact tracing depends on location-tracking possibilities embedded in the smartphone. If, say, police obtain access to the public health data, as has occurred in several places, including Singapore, the same data could be used for crime investigations as well as contagion control.

In the case of public health surveillance, then, the purposes are those mentioned by the WHO: disease prevention and control. Inevitably, this also includes control of people – who and where they are, who they are with and how close, physically. Another way of thinking about this is to say that surveillance occurs to make people visible in specific ways, then to represent them in those ways so that they can be treated appropriately for whatever purposes the surveillor has in mind. Thus, what *sorts* of data are collected, *how* they are analyzed, and *what* assessments and judgments are made from them are matters of moment – especially as the data is so sensitive, touching on matters of health and the body.

Public health data, then, might make people visible in terms of their relative ages – elderly people are generally more likely to become seriously ill or die if they contract COVID-19, for instance – or where they live – postcodes are often used as proxy for lifestyles by any and all of police, marketers and healthcare scientists – so that testing or vaccines can be targeted appropriately. Equally, public health agencies may wish to know who has been in contact with infected people, or whether those people are isolating or quarantining themselves, and surveillance may be sought for that quest.

Of course, several of these schemes turned out to be quite controversial, whether used for contact tracing or quarantine-policing or, on a large scale, for monitoring the progress of the mutating virus through large populations. Understandably, it is smartphone apps or wearables such as wristbands that directly affect individuals which raise most concern. For instance, a cluster of gay men was "outed" in South Korea when a number of COVID-19 cases came to light in a Seoul district well known for its gay bars. Also, a Minnesota law official appeared to claim that the state was using "contact tracing" to identify connections between Black Lives Matter protesters in May 2020.[4] But often the technologies used for surveillance have effects that are hard to discern by those whose data is in use, not least because their impact may be indirect.

As an example, in February 2020, South Korean citizens found that the government was publishing on websites and in texts the details of the exact movements of unidentified individuals for all COVID-19 cases. One could read, "Patient No. 12 had booked Seats E13 and E14 for a 5:30 pm showing of the South Korean film, 'The Man Standing Next.' Before grabbing a 12:40 pm train, patient No. 17 dined at a soft-tofu restaurant in Seoul."[5] Doubtless, the aim was to see whether undiscovered contacts could be traced and tested. But such data, in the wrong hands, could also be misused.

As well, *cultural* differences are significant – seen also, for instance, in the willingness to wear masks in public – in relation to allowing authorities to think that they can impose certain behavioral requirements or post personal details publicly. How people respond – for instance, by stigmatizing or even attacking those who fail to wear masks or who appear to have been contagion carriers – is another matter.

Context is critical

Although the H1N1 pandemic occurred in a world of information technology, the COVID-19 pandemic was the first to occur in a context of surveillance capitalism,[6] and this is crucially important. So-called Big Data had made its appearance in the early years of the twenty-first century, prompted by developments in distributed computing, data analytics and statistics. But its value for commerce, especially in rapidly expanding platform companies, following its signal success for Google and then several social media giants, was unprecedented.

Surveillance capitalism had discovered how to make profit from apparently inconsequential data exuded by these platforms, prompted by everyday users of platforms like Facebook and WeChat. But, crucially, that data could also be repurposed by, for example, police and security agencies. Governments found ways of using that data, too, and often sought to attract those large corporations to set up shop in their countries. An example is the attempt by Alphabet, Google's parent company, to plant a smart city in Toronto – "Sidewalk Labs."[7] The "smartness" lay in the data-dependence of the project, a high-tech "utopia" with sensors embedded everywhere. As the *Atlantic* put it, "The city is literally built to collect data about its residents and visitors."[8] The plan was aborted during the pandemic in May 2020.

It is clear that platforms were seeking yet other openings for obtaining valuable – and sensitive – data. Google's Deep Mind, an Artificial Intelligence (AI) company, built an app called Streams, for example, to give alerts to people with kidney injuries. But the Royal Free London National Health Service (NHS) Foundation Trust gifted 1.6 million patient-identifiable records to it in 2015, an act that contravened four data protection principles enshrined in British law, not to mention patient confidentiality.[9] It shows that platforms are keen to get their hands on such sensitive data and that some government-related bodies – in this case, the UK's NHS – seem willing to embed the likes of a Google subsidiary within their system, apparently without precautions.

Well before the pandemic, governments in many countries realized that they did not have the capacity to develop technologies deemed "necessary" for a digital era. Leaders such as IBM or some enterprising start-ups would engineer advances and then make agreements with governments. The Apple–Google collaboration, which followed this model, centered on an API – Application Programming Interface – that allows two applications to "talk" to each other. Used in several digital tracking apps for contact tracing, it does rely on "Privacy-Preserving" protocols, but this in itself does not mean that platforms such as Google would not like to obtain access to health data. As would governments. Contact tracing apps provide another government-sanctioned reason to have your phone send data over networks. This means more time-on-device which, as Shoshana Zuboff shows, is the raw material for platform companies.

The pandemic arrived in a context where (big) data was already prized for its apparent value in providing "solutions" in many areas of life, including in government. This is clear in other aspects of the pandemic context besides health and medicine. As lockdowns occurred, businesses, schools, stores – and doctors' offices, for that matter – went remote. There was a sudden massive demand for technology platform companies to continue work and education online. Zoom and others went into a boom phase, from 10 to 300 million users per day, between December 2019 and June 2020. Millions of people who were otherwise isolated from friends and family were thankful for the many video communication platforms that at least offered a chance for electronic connection. Surveillance capitalism – profiting from user attention data – was in its ascendance when the pandemic hit. The pandemic is a multi-faceted phenomenon.

This point is vital for any understanding of the COVID-19 pandemic. As an undergraduate student in the late 1960s, I read Albert Camus's *La Peste*,[10] a novel about a plague that broke out in Oran, Algeria in the 1940s. Although based on histories of a cholera epidemic that hit Oran in 1849, it describes in great detail the measures taken to try to contain the disease, firstly through the eyes of Bernard Rieux, the doctor who, when his building concierge caught a fever, first alerted the city to what was happening. Rats were dying in the streets and city workers had to clean them away and burn them – but that activity itself spread the infection. I never imagined, when I read the book as a student, that one day I would see something like this, only on a massive, international scale.

But what did I "see" as I watched the COVID-19 pandemic develop? I saw the *effects* of the pandemic in the *context* of an already existing set of public health practices learned most recently from SARS and H1N1, and of nationally varying on-the-ground activities. The latter depend heavily on the way in which governments-in-power work with technology platforms. This is surveillance capitalism, again. But Camus's tale also rings bells today.

In Oran, as during COVID-19, the authorities were slow to grasp the seriousness of the situation, bickering

10

over their response. Optimism was expressed in the official announcements, which led citizens to take the plague less seriously than was appropriate. Gradually, distancing was required and movement beyond the city restricted; hospital beds were set aside for victims but proved to be hopelessly insufficient. Likewise, when a serum was finally produced, supplies were far too small. In other words, *La Peste* is about a social, political and economic situation in a time of health crisis – with current resonance.

Interestingly, there are several epidemic accounts that are not dissimilar. Laura Spinney's 2017 book[11] about the "Spanish Flu" of 1918 – *Pale Rider* – describes the twentieth century's most devastating killer. This is a fine journalistic reconstruction of surprisingly underexplored terrain. The flu pandemic was caused – gene-sequencing showed, decades later – by a virus that mutated and jumped to humans from birds, something not understood until the 1990s. But here too, the social and geopolitical context is crucial. War had weakened soldiers, returning from several fronts, and lack of supplies meant widespread under-nourishment. The fatal flu outbreak killed more than 50 million across many countries worldwide, causing unimaginable and dire distress, and although several *cordons sanitaires*, restricting movement in specific areas, were established, they were too little, too late for many. Also, those most vulnerable were between the ages of 20 and 40.

The phenomena associated with the eruption of a highly contagious virus cannot be understood merely by scientific health and medical knowledge. The historical, geographical and cultural context, described by Spinney and by Camus – among many others – shows the importance of the multiple social dimensions of pandemics. And as Nurhak Polat rightly argues, in the early 2020s one cannot but examine the role of digital technologies in any attempt to understand COVID-19's manifold impacts. Therefore, she suggests – using "viral" in both actual and virtual senses – "Pandemics in the 21st century are inevitably embedded in the digital context. This also includes the digital and biometric surveillance technologies that track 'viral footprints' of COVID-19 across bodies, homes, streets, and borders."[12] In what follows, we shall consider the wearable trackers, phone apps, drones, remote body temperature checkers that have been sprung into service since COVID-19 began.

However, it is not enough just to discuss those digital technologies as they are applied to formal systems of surveillance, where all the emphasis is on how those systems bear down on "us," the objects of surveillance. This is because we, those surveillance objects, are also subjects of surveillance. While the apps, the cameras, the wearables "watch" us, we also glance slyly at each other – checking for masks, for 2-meter distance on sidewalks, for signs that neighbors are meeting with others beyond family. Moreover, the way we are classified – "no symptoms," "has received vaccine," "was exposed to a carrier" – may affect the way we see ourselves and watch, assess, interact with others, including how we measure our relationships with them. This is because today we develop new cultures of surveillance,[13] such that there's a "looping effect"[14] between the classifications and the people classified. Those classified not only classify others, but may modify their own activities due to their surveillance classification.

Pandemic and tech-solutionism

Almost all the proposed ways of dealing with the pandemic address only the symptoms, not the causes. They are Band-Aids, intended to contain and control the virus. At the time of writing, the original causes are not known to science, so the Band-Aid approach is understandable. Knowledge gleaned from many historical epidemics and pandemics informs how public health officials respond when new outbreaks occur. It is doubtful how much could be learned – except perhaps negatively – from the fourteenth-century Black Death, which killed huge swathes of the population around the Mediterranean. A wide variety of sometimes exotic treatments were proposed, from herbalism to blood-letting to self-flagellation, although doctors did learn to lance the bodily buboes that gave the disease its other name, "Bubonic Plague."

But – as in the case of the nineteenth- and, especially, twentieth-century epidemics such as the "Spanish Flu" – isolation and segregation of patients, along with the search for a serum, became common patterns. They worked with what was available in their day. So today, we work with what's available now. Keeping a physical distance – often misleadingly called "social distancing" – became commonplace, as did the need for mask-wearing and quarantine. And because ours is an era loaded with digital devices and systems

– not to mention global corporations successfully selling these – data and data analysis, plus Machine Learning and Artificial Intelligence, are seen as key COVID-containing contrivances.

Thus, in the early twenty-first century, the pressures pushing "technological solutionism"[15] are strong, and pandemic panic only adds further propulsion. As Rob Kitchin notes, those pressures include intense lobbying of governments by technology companies, their already-existing technocratic practices and their desire to stimulate high-tech innovation.[16] This was already visible in the rush to find "solutions" after the 2001 attacks on New York and Washington known as "9/11," when companies hastily used their home pages to offer simultaneous condolences to bereaved families and advertisements for their "anti-terrorism" products. And governments acceded, using techniques ranging from biometric tests to Artificial Intelligence to trace and impede terrorism.[17]

The same kind of response follows in other similar situations. It also happened, for instance, following the terrorist attacks on Mumbai – centring on the Taj Mahal Palace Hotel and the Railway Terminus – in 2008. Very quickly, both maritime security and hotel security – scanners, maritime identification systems, biometric IDs for fishermen – were enhanced with new surveillance measures, and new National Security Guard (NSG) units were deployed in major cities. These were "required" because the attack was mounted from the ocean, and due to delays with the NSG, which at the time was based only near New Delhi.[18] Today, in a *global* pandemic, such solutionism has a seductively powerful pull.

Why the haste to set up government security agencies and massive surveillance arsenals? Part of the answer is that citizens rightly demand adequate responses to emergencies and crises, by government. But Naomi Klein notes that another factor kicks in – the "shock doctrine."[19] She shows how governments frequently take advantage of both "natural" disasters and human conflicts to bring about major changes that consolidate their power. Klein now speaks of a "pandemic shock doctrine," clearly visible in New York Governor Andrew Cuomo's vision for a new New York, with Google and Microsoft "permanently integrating technology into every aspect of civic life."[20] Surveillance capitalism rides again.

Now, the point is emphatically not that high-tech products have no place in pandemic responses. It is, rather, that any such responses deserve to be checked for their fitness-for-purpose and their compliance with other priorities than health, such as privacy and civil liberties. Each digital offering has strict limits on what it can achieve, and each brings with it challenges as well as benefits to human life. Beyond this, it should also be acknowledged that such products are unlikely to *solve* pandemic problems. Rather, they are potential contri-butions to a tool-box of practices that, it is hoped, will mitigate some effects of the pandemic.

"Solutions" are considered in relation to dealing with causes more properly than merely with symptoms. As the "cause" of the COVID-19 pandemic is as yet unknown, dealing with that is more than moot.

However, one of the likely contributory factors relates to the fact that COVID-19, like many contemporary diseases, is zoonotic. That is, the virus jumps from animals to humans, as seems to have occurred in Wuhan. A 2020 UN conference on loss of biodiversity hinted strongly that the COVID-19 virus may be linked with – perhaps accelerated by – species depletion, itself related to, among other things, deforestation.[21] It is systemic. In contrast with the rapid rollout of new platforms, devices and apps, dealing with species depletion is a long-term, massive, planetary project. One might also continue the comparison with 9/11, in that the high-tech "solutions" introduced for national security purposes also ignored the deeper problems of the *cause* of terrorism in 2001.

The burden of this book

The burden of this book is that COVID-generated tech solutionism is creating digital infrastructures that tend to downplay negative effects on human life *and* are likely to persist into the post-pandemic world, endangering human rights and data justice. Many of the proposals and products that have circulated since early in 2020 are highly surveillant. That is, they depend on data that makes people visible in particular ways, representing them to other agents and agencies in those ways, so that those people can be treated accordingly.[22]

This is why "pandemic" and "surveillance" belong together. Indeed, the drive behind tech-solutionism suggests that at least two meanings may be given to "pandemic surveillance." One is the obvious existence of a range of surveillance initiatives prompted by the pandemic that invite critical investigation. The other is that these forms of surveillance have grown and mutated so rapidly that their spread might be thought of as "viral." In other words, there is a pandemic *of* surveillance.

Let me add a note about how we interpret and explain what is happening in the world of pandemic surveillance. Several perspectives are already evident in what has been said so far. One has to do with the connections between the human and the non-human world – I am thinking of the movement of the virus from animals to humans, in particular – that have such obvious relevance to the outcomes of the pandemic in general, and pandemic surveillance in particular. Another relates to the political economy of pandemic surveillance, in which corporations as well as government play a vital role in what sorts of surveillance occur, who benefits and who is negatively affected. The role of surveillance capitalism should not be underestimated.[23]

A third is what might be called a "biopolitical" perspective that emphasizes the ambiguity of power in pandemic surveillance. The power involved may be quite repressive, but it is also productive. Pandemic surveillance may lead to life-and-death decisions – who is "disposable?" asks Achille Mbembe.[24] But one cannot necessarily tell in advance what sorts of effects will be produced. Then a fourth perspective is "socio-technical," which looks particularly at the interplay between social and technical factors – especially the socially significant ways in which algorithms are produced, and also how they in turn have impacts on social situations.[25]

In what follows, I introduce some key themes of pandemic surveillance, chapter by chapter. I should say that, while I am convinced that what follows is a vital exercise – and I have learned a lot from my research – I also stress that what I have done is based very much on secondary sources, and on talking with those with expertise, as well as from personal participation in and observation of the pandemic. The pandemic is ongoing and some of its features, and responses to them, change over time. Nothing is fixed or solid.

I should also note that I write as someone who is a salaried white male, living in a city that has, to date, mainly been but lightly brushed – not brutally bombarded – by the pandemic. I acknowledge that this is a position of privilege and that I write having no first-hand personal experience of the desperate circumstances of many millions, worldwide, especially the colonized, racialized, the oppressed and the neglected. Talking and emailing with colleagues and friends in Australia, Brazil, China, Guatemala, Hong Kong, India, Japan, Israel/Palestine, Singapore, as well as closer to home in Canada and Europe, has given me some feel for others' realities.

Road-map *to* Pandemic Surveillance

"Disease-Driven Surveillance," chapter 2, takes us straight to what many think of as the heart of the issue: "contact tracing." While we do look carefully at such digital location tracking systems, set up to aid contact tracing, other apps, wearable devices and data systems have been used in the pandemic. For instance, vaccine passports – they go under various names – are being rolled out to enable access and travel for those who have received appropriate doses of one of the available vaccines. And then there are wearables, from electronic bracelets to an array of small devices such as Fitbits and Apple watches for checking body temperature and other data such as daily steps and sleeptime, that can detect pre-symptomatic cases of COVID-19.[26]

Then, much less visible but highly significant kinds of digital surveillance – health data networks – have been built for modeling what is happening within a given jurisdiction, so that trends may be mapped and resources targeted appropriately. These use massive databases, some set up for the purpose, for crunching numbers to track and monitor the spread of the virus and to predict its movement and the proportions likely to be affected. All these and more make up the panoply of digital surveillance that has proliferated since COVID-19 was identified.

Those directly "disease-driven" forms of surveillance are only part of the picture, however. The pandemic phenomenon touches all areas of life, spawning surveillance within each. Chapter 3, "Domestic Targets," discusses the dimensions beyond the obviously disease-driven. Residents of Kingston, where I live, were told to "stay home, stay safe" and that's just what happened. An astonishing domestic drift occurred, and suddenly our homes – already digitally wired in the global north – became surveillance sites as never before.

As well as the massively increased use of highly data-hungry platform companies that we use to keep in touch with those from whom we were suddenly separated, there were other modes of surveillance for monitoring employment, schooling and shopping at home. US companies Amazon and Walmart increased their profits by 56 percent in 2020, to total $10.7 billion. So far from the familiar notion that the home is a haven from prying eyes, providing a secure threshold from unwanted outside agencies, it became even more of a data-rich target.

Chapter 4, "Data Sees All?," dives into the world of data to discover why this abstract-sounding entity is so valued today. The pandemic hit in an era when data has become central to almost every facet of contemporary life. We explore how data is universally used as a "way of seeing" – while reminding ourselves that it is also a way of not-seeing. In this context, data is used to make our lives visible to others. Understandably, epidemiologists wish to know who has been with whom, where and for how long, and the data they collect and analyze allows them to "see" the lives of those in each community. But what might be missing from this?

Though many surveillors – especially platform companies – are not very transparent about what exactly they are doing, they make our lives very transparent to them. It is impossible for ordinary citizens to keep up with what data is being collected on them, especially now, with so many other pandemic preoccupations to deal with. It is not just a question of "collecting" data either. How that data is analyzed, using algorithms, is also crucial for outcomes. And those outcomes include being treated in a particular way, following the analysis. In China, if your color-coded situation obliges you to stay home, facial recognition camera surveillance or drones buzzing outside your apartment window make you even more visible to public health authorities.

These kinds of issues definitely raise questions about privacy, and they have to be faced squarely. But there are other sorts of questions here, that have to do with how populations are sorted into different categories – for example, for knowing which age-groups or work-positions should be vaccinated first. In Chapter 5, "Disadvantage and the Triage," these questions are investigated. When you go to an emergency department, you have to go through a "triage" process. The nurse on duty must sort out, on the basis of available information, which patients are in most urgent need of attention and care. Surveillance works like this – it sorts between different categories in the population so that different groups can be treated differently.[27]

COVID-19 has not only exposed how some populations are more vulnerable than others, and that there are inequalities of access to testing and vaccines. Pandemic surveillance also leads to variable treatment such that some experience very negative discrimination. Inequalities that have become very apparent – the disadvantages faced by people in poverty, migrant workers, visible minority groups – are sometimes also made even worse by pandemic surveillance. Questions of civil liberties and other rights are raised, nationally and globally.

Such issues prompt questions about power and how it is distributed. Chapter 6, "Democracy and Power," explores an upsurge of pandemic-prompted state surveillance, of which issuing "vaccine passports" is a good example. But we also have to face the fact that "state surveillance," which has for so long been the main worry for privacy advocates, is not the only kind evident in the COVID-19 global pandemic. Today's surveillance reveals itself in public–private partnerships – as is clear from the "contact tracing" apps that are nearly all products of *both* government and corporation, whether Huawei in China or IBM in the United States.

Of course, state and market can still be distinguished, but increasingly they are intertwined – including in their surveillance activities. The platform companies have ramped up their data-gathering during the pandemic. Many of these developments occurred in understandable haste, sometimes without adequate preparation – for public health initiatives, monitoring and checking on citizen compliance, and for stimulating demand for commercial pandemic services. Not only that, many are concerned that the seemingly temporary measures of intensified surveillance – sometimes enabled by changed regulations or laws – will become permanent features of society.

In the concluding chapter, "Doorway to Hope," threads are pulled together. The negative aspects of pandemic surveillance are not inevitable or inescapable. In a future pandemic, things could be done differently – and, indeed, lessons from COVID-19 could also be learned for a post-pandemic world. A major issue is the use of *data* within surveillance devices, apps and systems. "Tech-solutionism" is a palpable problem – there's more than one way to achieve results.

This book points to a different way, to start with people and public health, and not with technology. And if aspects of pandemic surveillance are unfair, then a different approach is to begin by aiming for "data justice." This is the quest for fairness in the ways in which people are made visible, represented and treated – and it's one of those things that makes possible human flourishing and the common good. This approach goes beyond privacy and also makes seeking alternatives everyone's business. Indeed, it strikes a note of hope, a doorway through which all may walk.

2
Disease-Driven Surveillance

Before the WHO recognized COVID-19 as a pandemic condition, public health officials had agreed on a common definition of what would count as a case of "infection with novel coronavirus (nCoV)."[1] Case counting is at the heart of disease-driven surveillance, and people worldwide have become used to news media presentations of daily case counts providing an indication of how different regions are doing in relation to each other. Where communicable disease is concerned, the work of counting cases is closely followed by trying to learn about which people may have been exposed through contact to these cases. This chapter concentrates mainly on contact tracing – and particularly contact tracing technologies, like contact tracing apps on mobile devices – because they help to highlight key questions about pandemic surveillance.

In April 2020, the Indian government launched a "contact-tracing, syndromic mapping and self-assessment tool" called Aarogya Setu. An open-source digital service, it was designed to run on Google's Android and Apple's iOS mobile operating systems. It enabled users to know when they had been close to others exposed to COVID-19, and to assess their own potential symptoms. This mobile app was installed more rapidly than Pokémon Go – 100 million times – in only 40 days. Even more rapidly, civil liberties and human rights objections to it were raised, very widely, often by those who had spent years trying to explain the downsides of Aadhaar, India's national biometric registration and identification system, launched in 2009.

The Kerala High Court received a petition in May 2020, stating that the app was unconstitutional and infringed on privacy. Not only the efficacy of such apps is debated, but also the fact that they collect, store and use sensitive personal data. Before it is used, petitioners said, its purposes should be limited, data minimized, and the data should be available only to specific departments. As set out, they noted, it lacked a legal framework and barriers to abuse.[2] So, while Aarogya Setu means "bridge to health" in Sanskrit, protesters insisted that it was really a bridge to more government surveillance, privacy would be in peril, and the government would become more authoritarian because of the compulsory character of Aarogya Setu. India is the only democracy to have made contact tracing apps mandatory.[3] However, it was never quite clear for *whom* they were required.

As in many other countries, digital contact tracing in India was seen as a potentially effective way of confronting the pandemic. But at the same time, for many, it rang warning bells about surveillance and privacy. As the technical initiative most widely used internationally, we begin with an examination of apps designed to assist in contact tracing. We shall focus on the comparisons and contrasts between centralized and mandatory systems – seen above all in China – on the one hand, and decentralized and voluntary systems, often facilitated by an unusual collaboration between Apple and Google, on the other. A good question to ask, however, is how different these supposedly contrasting systems are.

Contact tracing is only one of many surveillant responses spawned by the pandemic. Large-scale public health data-modeling and epidemiological tracking also occur to try to track the geographical and social course of the virus as a guide to how health professionals and facilities might be deployed, and the public guided about appropriate protections and behaviors during the pandemic. These also appear in this chapter, along with reference to specific COVID-19 devices and systems – such as drones, facial recognition technology, thermal cameras and wearables – that have played a prominent part in some countries. Many such digital initiatives depend on public–private partnerships for funding and instruction-on-use, which also raises questions about surveillance and government. And, as vaccines roll out – notably, first in the world's rich countries – and travel once again becomes a possibility, immunity passes or vaccine passports appear. Disease-driven surveillance expands, then, at each stage and in many dimensions of the pandemic.

Disease-Driven Surveillance

Contact tracing and location-tracking apps

Contact tracing is a tried-and-tested method of discovering who may have been exposed to a virus and, beyond that, of working out the path and speed of spread of an epidemic. A common scenario is this: individuals known to be infected are interviewed to determine where they were exposed to illness (trace back) and whom they possibly have infected once in their infectious period (trace forward). This enables workers to identify all cases in a cluster and prevent further transmission through steps like quarantine of exposed individuals. It is a meticulous and sometimes cumbersome – and even, in some places, risky – process in the midst of a rapidly developing health crisis. But this manual method continues to prove its worth.

However, when the Ebola outbreak occurred in sub-Saharan Africa in 2014, the WHO introduced a new digital system to facilitate the task. Using a mobile phone, a health worker such as Léa Kanyere, in Goma, could take the temperature of people in an affected zone, record details and pass them on to her supervisor in the city, promptly and with less fear of suspicion or opposition.[4]

The COVID-19 pandemic hit a world seemingly awash with digital devices, so it comes as no surprise that many saw those devices – primarily phones – as likely anti-virus tools. Digital location tracking apparently offered an adjunct to the conventional public health practice of manual contact tracing. This conviction prompted a global rush to find a suitable means of linking phone use with attempts to contain the pandemic.

High-rise, high-tech Singapore was first to come up with a "TraceTogether" app, developed with advice from public health authorities, and uptake was rapid. In the first ten days, almost 20 percent of the population installed the voluntary app. But people quickly found that the app drained their cellphone battery. Then it was realized that few of Singapore's migrant workers, from India, Pakistan and Bangladesh, had smartphones, thus compromising the effectiveness of the system,[5] and that police had access to the data.[6]

Ordinary people, trying to keep their lives together in the midst of an unprecedented crisis outside their lived experience, seem willing to try many things. Fear of contagion meets public goodwill. But if you need to conserve your batteries to check on your elderly mother, or if you're all too aware of your friendly Bangladeshi cleaner working in your apartment block and the construction workers in the street outside, whom you pass on your way to meet your kids coming home from school, app-use participation may pall. Everyday cultures make a difference to technology adoption.

Whether or not the app "works" also depends on many other factors, and situations differ from country to country. Much participation was voluntary – even, in the end, in countries such as India. If you wished to be mobile, due to your responsibilities, contact tracing was usually required. But technically, too, the hastily developed apps differed from each other, also affecting their effectiveness.

Understandably, given the lack of experience of a global pandemic, a primary concern is with the health of one's own family and community and thus with what can be done to stay healthy and to limit the spread of the virus. "Contact tracing apps" might work. However, the pandemic arrived not only in a digital context, but in a world where the platform companies had gained great power as well as wealth. This became visible in the ways that governments have had a hard time reining them in – think of scandals such as the Cambridge Analytica affair in 2018, for instance, where democratic elections had been jeopardized by Facebook data use[7] – and also in the way that governments actively seek to attract them as partners. Disputes between governments and tech corporations often center on questions of surveillance and privacy. But partnerships between them depend on mutual benefits – put crudely, economic advantages for regions and access to more data for the companies.

There are other factors at work as well. For instance, the "digital" does not produce itself, however much some platform companies like to give the impression that they are an unstoppable force. Another factor is this: ever since the Second World War, a military logic has helped – ironically – to shape today's healthcare, especially when a global "threat" rears its "hostile" head. Indeed, the first use of the word "surveillance" in relation to healthcare was by Alexander Langmuir, who began work at the Centers for Disease Control and Prevention in 1949. He drew on his war-time service with the Department of Defense Committee on Biological Warfare to frame and attract funding for disease surveillance. His definition of this was clarified in a 1963 Harvard lecture.

As Martin French observes, this "engenders a kind of surveillance focused so heavily on disease that the broader determinants of health are left out of the picture."[8] Such social factors include income, education, the physical environment, plus experiences such as discrimination, racism and historical trauma.[9] Not only twentieth-century war, but also 9/11 and the ensuing "war on terror," reinforced this pattern, stimulating the insertion of security into healthcare delivery, especially in the US. Hospitals and healthcare professionals thus "require" new investment in technology and infrastructure as solutions to events such as pandemics.[10] Perhaps this also helps to explain the relative lack of transparency in some pandemic healthcare data initiatives.[11]

With COVID-19, governments and public health authorities around the world were suddenly faced with a new situation, a global pandemic of unparalleled magnitude, outstripping the severity of the ghastly "Spanish Flu" of just over a century before, and the scope of more recent MERS, SARS and H1N1 epidemics. Much laudable activity took place as governments consulted with medical and health researchers and officials, following the WHO's declaration of a "public health emergency of international concern" on January 30, 2020. Just three weeks later, infection rates and deaths surged in Italy, followed quickly by the first COVID death in Brazil: someone newly returned from Italy.[12] At the same time, more than half the world's COVID victims were dramatically stranded on the *Princess Diamond* cruise ship in Yokohama, Japan, from which crucial early lessons about lockdown were learned.[13] And just a month later, Singapore released its TraceTogether Bluetooth app, the joint production of the Government Technology Agency and the Ministry of Health.[14]

Very soon afterwards, other countries, lacking a government technology agency like Singapore's, capable of developing an app, started working with tech companies. In China, it was a collaboration between Alipay and WeChat that produced the three-colored Health Code app at the end of February 2020. Participation was required of all citizens. Along with alerting smartphone owners to their possible contact with infected others, the system apparently shared data with the police as well.[15] But then, such sharing also occurred, for a time, in my home province of Ontario, as well as elsewhere in Canada.[16]

Was this also the opportunity for a new level of automated state surveillance? We shall see. Meanwhile, the large-scale Western initiative was based on a contrasting offer from Google and Apple to provide an API, enabling widespread decentralized location tracking for contact tracing. This was first piloted in Switzerland in late May 2020. These unlikely partners focused on privacy and interoperability, leaving local bodies to develop the apps themselves. In the case of the Google–Apple Exposure Notification (GAEN), the onus is on the user to follow up an alert; personal data is not sent to health authorities.

Evaluations of the GAEN system will continue to be made for a long time but its very appearance raises a number of big questions. Among these is the basic issue of what *should* be the relationship between tech businesses and government public health agencies? As Teresa Scassa notes, "The most challenging issues were

31

privacy and trust ... which affected app design and government choices."[17] While the Google–Apple system is in some ways less useful for public health – for instance, because no data goes to the system either for follow-up or for disease modeling – its privacy features seem to have contributed to more take-up due to increased user trust. How ordinary citizens perceive surveillance makes a difference.

All manner of tech "solutions" could be proposed, but the more sophisticated ones tend to be less supportive of human rights, privacy and trust. Hence GAEN's emphasis on "exposure" rather than "contact," on decentralized data storage, and data deletion after 14 days. GAEN also works better with Apple devices than other systems, which also makes it more attractive to some government bodies. It remains to be seen how the normative implications of the GAEN-based apps are worked out, especially in contexts where public health authorities might have wanted more usable data.

Contrasting contact tracing systems

Part of the attraction of a smartphone is that it "knows" where it is. Its location is recorded within the device, such that any movement is also tracked. Pandemic contact tracing is a painstaking process that requires much manual labour, so the idea of automating the process through digital location tracking will clearly be attractive to public health officials, especially during a speedily spreading and highly infectious disease. However, one possible drawback is that the smartphone is also the key component of contemporary surveillance systems.[18] Contact tracing and exposure notification apps add another layer to an already surveillance-heavy device.

Surveillance is frequently understood in literal terms of being watched by someone in authority – for example, police or security agencies. Thus, the video camera, mounted on buildings and street poles, or in workplaces, stores and transit stations, became the iconic image of surveillance in the twentieth century. However, a much better "image" for surveillance in the twenty-first century is the smartphone. Today, the watching is no longer primarily literal, as with a camera; surveillance is achieved primarily through *data*. And a key connector between persons and their surveillors is the phone – which is why I often refer to the smartphone as a PTD, a Personal Tracking Device, something that many people, especially in the world's richer countries, carry in their pockets, as kind of extensions of our bodies, hands and eyes.

In the previous chapter, I defined surveillance in what could be called a top-down manner.[19] But I have also proposed that surveillance be considered as "the operations *and experiences* of gathering and analyzing personal data for influence, entitlement or management."[20] Today, we are "watched" by data, or by *using* data. We are increasingly *aware* that the platform companies, such as Facebook and Google, know an awful lot about us.[21] The banner ads on our screens frequently refer to recent searches that we have conducted or activities we have pursued, demonstrating that they have tabs on us. Netflix and Amazon also draw our attention to movies, books and other products that often *do* reflect our interests.

What was once considered as primarily the realm of national security or policing is now also done by consumer corporations and, of course, by many other government departments. Surveillance is also engaged to keep track of matters such as healthcare, which is why there is further confusion and controversy in the time of pandemic. It makes sense to try to check on the progress of the pandemic by tracking its movements across countries, between cities and, most importantly, within cities, where the population is most densely distributed. Systems such as contact tracing apps bridge the divide between, on one hand, the statistics describing the spread of disease, and, on the other, the actual people who have contracted or might contract COVID-19.

South Korea was an early adopter of contact tracing apps, based on their experience with another epidemic, MERS, in 2015. From that time, a law already existed allowing authorities to use data from credit cards, mobile phones and CCTV for the purpose of tracking disease outbreaks. But the Center for Disease Control had to warn against too much information being published about people's movements. For example, someone was wrongly accused of having an affair with his sister-in-law when their overlapping maps suggested they'd had a restaurant date.[22]

Contact tracing is a painstaking process. It works most effectively when infections are still rare, and when testing is readily available to all. But in a world where consumers have been taught that "there's an app for that," automating the manual process seems attractive.[23] Many contact tracing schemes use apps that inform others who have recently been close – say, within 2 meters for 15 minutes – to an infected person. Singapore's TraceTogether system, for instance, began hopefully, with public health criteria to the fore, but did not pass the critical 60 percent take-up rate required for full functionality until its use was required in supermarkets and workplaces.[24]

At least three kinds of questions may be asked about these systems. One, obviously, enquires about how well they work. While this is a vitally important question, the jury will be out for quite a while on their real usefulness for public health. And, clearly, digital contact tracing can at best only be seen as an adjunct to other forms of contact tracing, and in relation to factors such as the availability of tests and vaccines. One study, for instance, examined results from China, Germany, Italy, Singapore, South Korea and the US, thus covering both centralized and decentralized systems.[25]

The cautious results of this study, which acknowledged difficulties such as different reporting styles and varying geographical and cultural differences that could affect the outcomes, was a guarded optimism about the effectiveness of contact tracing apps. However, the authors could only comment, even then, on the positive *correlation* between using contact tracing and a reduction in COVID-19 infections. A causal relationship could not be established. Other studies are less positive. And even this one stressed that their analysis could not evade questions of civil liberties, damage to which may be an unacceptable cost of digital contact tracing.

But, while the efficacy of digital contact tracing is

patently critical, a second question focuses on issues of surveillance, privacy and people's rights. Rob Kitchin wisely warned early on that, even before their fitness-for-use had been established, contact tracing apps presented "significant implications for civil liberties, governmentality and citizenship."[26] And he refuted the notion that public health trumps civil liberties. For one thing, the technologies may not deliver. Two, to trade civil liberties for health is a tech solutionist position, where it is believed that only technology can help, or that, even if flawed, technology can *still* help. This simply creates a scenario where, either way, the technology must be used. Thirdly, another option is available, to work for technology *and* civil liberties. We return to these issues in chapter 6.

Yet another set of questions relates to degrees of centralization involved in the various systems, which poses further queries about what kind of government is emerging, which will in turn affect both previous questions of surveillance consequences and of efficacy in reining-in the virus. This is discussed at greater length here.

The main Chinese system, Health Code, is highly centralized, and the Google–Apple API (GAEN), at the other extreme, decentralized. Each of these can be described in terms of the basic contrast between the mandatory, centralized systems and the voluntary, decentralized ones. There are other centralized schemes than the Chinese system, such as in South Korea, Israel and Qatar, whereas there are at least 50 decentralized GAEN ones, from Panama, Poland and Portugal to Slovenia, South Africa and Spain. There are also centralized systems – such as in Australia and Alberta, Canada – that require consent from users.

Centralized contact tracing

In China, where the pandemic probably began, things moved rapidly from the start. As early as mid-January, someone – we'll call her Xiaodan – infected with COVID-19 entered the public transit system in Nanjing, using several trains and buses, and potentially exposing others to the pathogen en route. The trips took more than two hours on one day and nearly two hours on the next, but the pervasive surveillance system was able to track to the minute where Xiaodan boarded and alighted from each train and bus. Details were immediately posted on social media and Nanjing residents were warned to go for tests if they had been in the same station, train or bus as Xiaodan.[27]

The Health Code contact tracing apps that followed in February were soon in more than 200 cities and quickly became commonplace. You could walk up to the store, pull up the app, scan a QR code and wait for your temperature to be taken.[28] When you see the green light on your phone you proceed into the store. Same again when you exit. If your light is yellow, you must self-quarantine at home. If red, you have to go into supervised quarantine. Drones, CCTV, facial recognition systems, electronic payment location data and thermal cameras are also used for checking up on quarantine and self-isolation. The Health Code is mandatory for all wishing to visit public places or going to workplaces in more than 300 cities. A green code is required for travel using public transit, in schools, restaurants, airports, hotels and grocery stores.

The Health Code system assesses the risk of viral infection based on travel histories, time spent in risky zones and contact with potential carriers. By October 2020, the Health Code was used in at least 300 cities, covering 900 million transmissions. According to Fan Liang,[29] it is based on three factors. One, personal information such as name, ID number, facial recognition registration and health condition – fever, cough and the like, which has to be updated daily. Two, place-and-time as recorded by the platforms, Alipay and WeChat, in daily routine GPS use, to check how risky areas visited are and how long the possible exposure. Three, Health Code calculates the likelihood of contact with virus-carriers based on user networks and online transactions. The additional feature, already seen in the first example in Nanjing, is mapping, which became the task of another platform, Baidu. The COVID-19 map shows the location and numbers of confirmed cases in many Chinese cities.

While China leads the world in the compulsory use of digital contact tracing apps – and was also able to reduce the number of lockdowns and potential deaths much earlier than many countries – others have also chosen to depend heavily on such systems. I should also observe that the Chinese system involves much more than contact tracing. It exists within a more complex suite of surveillance technologies, in a country where both government and commercial surveillance are more deeply entrenched, integrated and evident in everyday life.

South Korea is another highly data-dependent country, whose approach was early and aggressive, using cellphone alerts and social media posts to warn of locations visited by people infected by COVID-19. It, too, used disease surveillance beyond contact tracing, but the mix led to some predictable stigmatizing of certain population groups and individuals. Taiwan and Hong Kong also used GPS and Wi-Fi to track infected individuals. Bahrain's and Kuwait's centralized systems informed governments of the locations of infected people.[30] Israel launched a "Hamagen" app – meaning "shield" – but also enlisted Shin Bet, its security spying agency, to monitor phones under an emergency powers order. Pakistan, too, used its intelligence services, employing secretive insurgent-locating technology, to track COVID-19 victims and their contacts.

Decentralized contact tracing
Right from the start of the pandemic, when digital contact tracing tools were mooted, democratically minded commentators stressed the need to avoid centralized and mandatory systems. They worried about the potential for government overreach and for surveillance "function creep" – that is, the use of surveillance technologies for other purposes than those for which they were designed.

In June 2020, the Canadian government announced that it was supporting a smartphone app to alert those who had been near someone who had tested positive for COVID-19.[31] An exposure-notification app was developed by a group affiliated with Ottawa-based Shopify. As in nearly 50 other jurisdictions, it relies on the API provided by the joint efforts of Apple and Google. Blackberry Corporation took responsibility for security review – data leaks and attacks being the main fears – of the app, eventually launched as "COVID-Alert." Its use is voluntary, its usefulness depends in part on the uptake rate, and it remains blind to unreported cases, which in some areas are significant.

The Federal and Ontario Privacy Commissioners signaled some concerns with the app but gave it qualified approval.[32] The Canadian system offers an anonymous alert, the data is decentralized within users' phones, and kept for only 14 days. As a Bluetooth device, the app notes only *that* someone has been close to an infected person, and not *where* that encounter occurred. Many believe that the Bluetooth options are better protectors of privacy. The somewhat more skeptical Canadian NGOs dealing with digital rights and freedoms concurred generally with the Privacy Commissioners, while withholding judgment on some matters.[33]

Unsurprisingly, this mixed message about the Canadian system was more than matched in some other countries. An MIT "Covid Tracing Tracker" captures details of every significant contact tracing system in the world, scoring each, in particular, for its concern with civil liberties.[34] Democracies, they say, use more safeguards than other polities. But one thing the MIT tracker doesn't show is whether or not what they call democracies do less surveillance than others. However, such analyses remain at a relatively superficial level. Basic questions still remain about the "Western" decentralized and voluntary contact tracing systems, the primary one of which draws attention to a key similarity between the Chinese and GAEN systems: their common reliance on platforms.

Problems with platforms

The role of digital platforms is critically important in *both* centralized and decentralized types of contact tracing. As Liang stresses, the Chinese platforms serve both to mediate state–citizen relationships, and also to render citizens in a state of ongoing visibility. This happens more clearly and ineluctably in the Chinese case, but in some ways this also describes aspects of the Western, decentralized cases, too. In China, the government allows the commercial tech giants to collect massive amounts of sensitive data, which can also be shared with police.[35]

Also, as Liang points out, the platforms are "pivotal gatekeepers in the data-flows." Together, Alipay and WeChat track a widening range of users' daily activities. Alipay also supplies electronic IDs for obtaining access to government services, and offers technical support and data sources for Big Data policing. In China, constant classification and ranking of the population occurs through social media as well as through government-led social credit systems. Health Code could be seen as just one more platform-assisted form of rating and ranking citizens. Ordinary people become more and more transparent to a mix of government and commercial operations, which in return are hardly transparent to them.

Meanwhile, the GAEN option allowed for many countries to develop their own decentralized digital tracking systems, using local platforms, as described for the Canadian case. However, as we have seen, the issues are far too complex to reduce the range of contact tracing/ exposure-notification to either/or, or even to a spectrum from one "extreme" to another. Each jurisdiction has to be understood in its own political-economic and cultural context.

One day, the story of that huge global enterprise will be written and discussed, perhaps even as a pivotal point in relationships between governments and corporations. Of course, such mutual dependence has been growing steadily, in part from its military origins in the post-war period and the further boost from 9/11.[36] But the pandemic prompted platform corporations to greater boldness in their offers to assist the global efforts to mitigate and repel COVID-19. While many individuals involved in these efforts were undoubtedly public-spirited, and even compassionate, it is as platform *companies* that they are discussed here.

Some consider independent apps and those built on the GAEN initiative as purveyors of "corporate contact tracing."[37] They refer to it this way because of the infrastructure behind the contact tracing or exposure notification initiatives. This includes the privately owned Apple and Android devices, with their proprietary and open-source operating systems, the telecommunication companies with their data plans, and the "data miners who extract and commercialize data from this information ecosystem." The concern of these analysts is the apparent threat to the very idea of *public* health from the fundamental involvement of these corporations, whose operations have clearly been shown to contribute to social inequality through "discriminatory design and algorithmic oppression."

After all, as French and others also show, it was only in 2015 that the UK scandal blew up regarding identifiable data being transferred, without patient consent, from the Royal Free London NHS Foundation Trust to Google DeepMind. It also led to doubts being expressed in 2020 about the UK NHS app, on the grounds of its very weak data and privacy controls. But the further issue is that oversight of all corporate data systems is hardly possible due to the sheer opaqueness of many such systems. And, as Frank Pasquale[38] and others have argued, this is a "black box" issue – in the sense of their often being based on hidden algorithms. This is discussed further in chapter 4.

However, it also appears that the UK NHS contact tracing app did make a distinct difference to the course of the pandemic. Thousands of deaths were prevented, say researchers, along with hundreds of thousands of cases.[39] It was "used regularly" by 16.5 million people, or 28 percent of the UK population. This conflicts with the view expressed earlier in 2021 by the UK House of Commons Public Accounts Committee that it had made "no measurable difference."

For all these reasons, contact tracing apps have been front-and-center of debates over pandemic surveillance, around the world. And, while it is likely that, in a general sense, "the COVID-19 pandemic is the context that will shape the ongoing competition between China and the US,"[40] the COVID-19 pandemic will likely also prompt further debate on the relative merits of centralized and decentralized modes of organizing public health measures such as digital contact tracing. Not only has the US fared far worse in terms of deaths per thousand – assuming that the figures in either country are reliable – China's digital public health measures, though in some ways draconian, also saved many lives. And, at the time of writing, it is impossible to know how far the current surveillance systems will persist into post-pandemic times.

Beyond contact tracing

The main thrust of this chapter is to highlight debates over contact tracing, regarding their public health efficacy. Later chapters delve into the question of their contribution to surveillance, inequality and increased government control. However, various other surveillance apps and devices have been used in an effort to limit the spread of the pandemic. These include the use of drones, CCTV and facial recognition systems to police quarantine, and wearables – such as a "bio-button" introduced after protests against its original mandatory status at Oakland University[41] to check symptoms such as skin temperature, or wristbands for similar purposes – and, of course, the vaccine passes for permitting travel for those who have been vaccinated.

The vaccine passes did not begin to appear until after the vaccines themselves had been developed but, given the pandemic-repressed desire among many to travel, or to enter cinemas, gyms and workplaces, their arrival was not surprising. Sometimes called "Vaccine passports," in which their association with travel is evident, some were already in use by March 2021 – for instance, in Israel, which introduced "green passes" early, once more than 50 percent of the Israeli population had been vaccinated. Those holding passes could enter gyms, theatres and restaurants. Both China and the European Union also developed similar passes quite early. IBM has promised to develop a pass, and a "Commons Project" is working on a system for documenting vaccinations. A smartphone app is also promised from IATA, the International Air Transport Association. Clearly, if anyone requires vaccine passports, it is the travel industry, and if they are developed, they will have to be internationally approved.

But these passes are not without their downsides. If the governments in rich countries start to use passes, they could contribute to pandemic extension, just because of the fragmented nature of their global rollout. A relevant map of the world quickly reveals how poorly distributed vaccines are in less developed countries. Moreover, to work effectively, international agreement would be required, which is unlikely, given the variety of vaccines and the fact that they are not approved for use in all countries – for instance, the AstraZeneca vaccine, used in 86 countries, has yet to be approved for use in the US. The Chinese vaccine passport scheme will admit to China only those who have received a Chinese vaccine.[42]

Vaccine passes raise questions about the integrity of the data on which their use is predicated and what safeguards are in place to ensure data is protected. And, where vaccination varies with racialized groups – such as Black and Latino people in the US – already-present inequalities will multiply. Producing an internationally accepted vaccine passport cannot be done overnight; after all, the international passport system took 50 years to complete. As a digital system, associated with a phone, there are many issues of data confidentiality and security to be overcome – and the stakes are high.[43]

Public health information systems

It is one thing, however, to discuss some specific digital technologies that have been used in the COVID-19 pandemic; another to consider what coordination and data-sharing occurs on a large scale. If public health authorities are to make appropriate policy, they need meaningful information input at the level of the whole population. Those health apps and devices, if they have proved to produce reliable data, work most effectively when they are connected with public healthcare systems at large.[44] Such systems have expanded over many years, often changing direction or adding more features as medical and epidemiological knowledge has developed. Interestingly, in some cases they have also changed their character by learning from large-scale data operations in another sphere – that of national security.[45]

For public health responses to be equal to a pandemic, timely, reliable and robust information is required. Public health information management involves many stages, from initial data collection, through verifying and analyzing data, to disseminating the relevant information to those public health professionals who need it. During the pandemic, many people have checked their local public health statistical charts on a daily basis. Thus, publics in many countries have become aware of the significance of modeling – analyzing the spread of the virus and predicting its movement using health, geographic and other data.

This has become a major surveillance operation for COVID-19, as public health data is being used in novel ways to grasp pandemic realities. And, once more, government-sponsored public health systems also rely heavily on private companies and private–public partnerships for data analysis and interpretation. Important issues are raised at every level, about what data is collected and how it is curated, to the algorithms developed for the analysis, through to how exactly that data is used, and by whom. The use of race-based data is clearly controversial for just these reasons.

For example, in the UK, the National Health Service quickly assembled NHSX, a public health platform developed for the pandemic, to allow others to make informed and effective decisions about the allocation of personnel, equipment and resources.[46] The NHSX works with Microsoft, Palantir, Amazon Web Services, Faculty – an AI specialist company – and Google. This is a public–private partnership that includes not only some well-known and generally reputable companies, but also some others – such as Palantir, whose reputation has been tarnished by associations with the CIA, with the Trump Administration's crackdown on immigration, and predictive policing.[47] Palantir, a Silicon Valley company named after the seeing stones in

J. R. R. Tolkien's *The Lord of the Rings*, has been hired by several countries embroiled in the pandemic.[48] Its presence, predictably, is problematic to many.

China also runs very large-scale data platforms in response to the pandemic, and these have helped tremendously in predicting, tracking and planning for the spread of the contagion. But even those reports that praise the use of Big Data analytics for their assistance in containing the pandemic also acknowledge problems at several levels, including data quality and data protection. For the former, data standards were not uniform, among other things, leading to untimely reporting in situations where speed of response was of the essence. In the latter, the system was shown to have inadequate privacy protection and "undisclosed compliance risks." It was also noted that people leaving Wuhan to visit their home villages were exposed online, causing unwarranted harassment, intimidation and physical threats.[49]

More broadly, the public health systems developed for the pandemic thrust into view basic questions of trust in governments to do the right thing. Google and Apple, who offered government bodies the infrastructure for contact tracing apps, still set the rules for their production.[50] Governments have long had access to health data, along with statistical data about populations. But what about location data, now routinely used by numerous platforms? Should governments take advantage of the availability of such very revealing and socially sensitive data during a public health crisis? These questions are critical, especially in a time of mushrooming surveillance.[51]

Surveillance surge

Sometimes surveillance grows slowly, steadily, imperceptibly, and at other times, particular events give it a sudden boost, and surveillance surges.[52] In the early 2020s, the COVID-19 pandemic is the trigger for an unprecedented surveillance surge. This sudden swelling of surveillance is flood-like, arriving rapidly and unexpectedly, threatening, like the pandemic itself, to inundate whole societies. Its liquidity[53] has been facilitated, in recent decades, by the increasing potential for data to flow not only within organizations but between them. The internet, using submarine and underground cables, and accessed by personal devices, stretches this to a global – even, given the negative effects on the earth itself, a planetary – level,[54] due not least to the power of the platforms that generate so much of the data-flow.

The examples used thus far indicate clearly how the pandemic is not only a *medical* or a *health* condition but also a social, economic and profoundly political condition. In his book, *Discipline and Punish*, French philosopher Michel Foucault famously linked responses to eighteenth-century plagues with the rise of more disciplinary governments.[55] This was before he discussed the "Panopticon," Jeremy Bentham's brain-child – the all-seeing prison design. *The Economist* worried about this early in the pandemic – warning that a "*Coronopticon*" could appear.[56] Pandemic surveillance could become "all-seeing." Bentham's prisoners, one might say, were supposed to self-discipline for fear of authority; in the Coronopticon, many self-discipline for fear of disease and death.

But is this really the only or best way of exploring pandemic surveillance? Foucault's preliminary case for understanding surveillance was not the prison but the *plague-town*. Stuart Eldon shows how this makes a better exemplar of today's surveillance societies than the Panopticon.[57] After all, in Foucault's account, "This surveillance [of the plague-town] is based on a system of permanent registration: reports from syndics to intendants and from the intendants to the magistrates or mayor."[58] Replay this in a digital key and it sounds a lot like what I describe in this book. It is undoubtedly the case that the pandemic is pushing surveillance into a whole new phase, the character of which has yet to become completely clear.

Some things are taking shape, however. The notion of "disease-driven surveillance" takes on a new meaning when considered in light of the security-oriented origins of public health surveillance. Though humans are the carriers and sufferers, public health surveillance is intended to be of the *disease*. As hinted earlier, this may mean that broader social determinants of health are less than visible to the initiators of the surveillance.

As we shall see, this leads to possible failures of pandemic surveillance to notice either the contrasting material conditions of different groups affected by the pandemic or, still less, the ways in which the actual reinforcement of such inequitable conditions may be a product of the surveillance. Put another way, those acting in the name of public health could miss seeing some inequalities of pandemic response, and its surveillance may even create new forms of uneven treatment. This theme is picked up in chapters 4–5.

Disease-Driven Surveillance

Unless we're directly affected through infection, however, the way the majority of people *experience* a pandemic is primarily through lockdowns and business closures – not to mention, for the middle classes, spending much time at home. These not only limit our "normal" activities and behavior – the source of much disappointment and frustration – they are also a further means by which pandemic surveillance swells. As a social condition, the pandemic also brings surveillance home, sometimes in dramatically new ways. In particular, working, shopping, learning and seeking entertainment at home opens the digital door to multiple monitoring by employers, stores, schools and platform companies. This is investigated in the next chapter.

3
Domestic Targets

In our city, the brightly lit signs on the front of buses and numerous roadside "temporary conditions" signs read, "Stay Home, Stay Safe." We are urged, and repeatedly reminded, to go home, stay home and be safe. Most heed the call. Many millions of people, worldwide, did indeed stay home, if they could. Healthcare workers and other essential services and businesses were excepted, but, for many, the pandemic is experienced above all – and in unusual ways – domestically. And the public health verdict, universally, is that staying home proved to be a key means of reducing the ravages of contagion.

But staying safe? Well, yes, it was definitely safer from the point of view of evading infection to remain behind those walls. But there were also levels of unsafety that rose behind doors. Domestic violence, mental health deterioration and other social difficulties occurred in the "haven" of home. But a much more silent intruder also slipped into that space – surveillance. Of course, this was nothing new. In richer countries, the domestic realm has been particularly targeted by advertisers and influencers ever since the rise of geo-demographic marketing in the 1990s. But with the pandemic, many "external" relationships, with employers, companies and schools, became internal. Surveillance came home with a vengeance.

Some of that discipline and surveillance was directly health-related. For example, parents had to juggle responsibilities as children were tested for COVID-19 each time they had a fever or cough. Elderly people living at home were frequently bereft of familiar forms of companionship, not to mention – like many of us – baffled by the changing and often confused novel rules of contact. Who could enter the home was restricted to regular household groups with some leeway for others in regular "bubbles." And even at home, certain interactions – such as when someone came to repair plumbing or adjust internet connections – demanded distancing, face-masks, hand sanitizer and other extraordinary risk-reducing measures. All understandable, under the circumstances, but bizarre aberrations from what, for many, was "normal" domestic life.

Life in multiple dimensions converged on the domestic realm, as workplaces, schools and stores closed, along with cinemas, theatres, places of worship, sports arenas, community centers and gyms. Also, Zoom came into its own, along with many other video-communication platforms, offering alternatives to being face-to-face with family and friends, and providing precious life-lines to the lonely and neglected. And with each came its own surveillance. The public world squeezed into the private one bringing with it its own idiosyncratic priorities – yet more passwords to remember – demands, checks, rules and expectations. In particular, home became the locus of work, school and shopping, not to mention leisure pursuits.

Reflecting on emergency procedures during the seventeenth-century plague, Foucault described this as a – perverse – utopia of a "perfectly governed city." He commented on the "plague-stricken town, traversed throughout with hierarchy, surveillance, observation, writing – the town immobilized by the functioning of an extensive power that bears in a distinct way over all individual bodies."[1] Foucault pictures the town, with its accustomed movements restricted – "everyone ordered to stay indoors … a segmented, immobile, frozen space. Each individual is fixed in his place … Inspection functions ceaselessly."[2]

Thanks to digital technologies, however, the COVID-19 "plague" *also* allows many contemporary equivalents of Foucault's "inspectors," "militia" and "guards"[3] right inside the home. Back in the twentieth century, the home had been declared a space into which the state should not intrude. Indeed, the 1948 Universal Declaration of Human Rights makes clear that "No one shall be subjected to arbitrary interference with his privacy, family … home."[4] Feminist queries about how far such a right should go, given persistent patterns of domestic violence, are vitally important, and well taken. But doesn't the fact that government departments – plus, now, commercial agencies with their own powers of classification and treatment – can "enter" homes with apparent impunity raise questions about an erasure of rights?

The pandemic, and with it some new surveillance developments, is a novel social and cultural condition, brought about by the declaration of a public health crisis. Not only are plague-type constraints in place, modifying mobility and focusing life-activities in the home as well as outside it. But, also, those life-activities are themselves monitored domestically by remote external bodies. Further, self-surveillance for symptoms and mutual surveillance for compliance are encouraged in many places. These activities too have been digitized, such that a smartphone – along with other compatible devices – becomes a means of fulfilling each function.

Under what used to be thought of as normal circumstances, if you are at work or in school, you likely have an ID whereby your activities may be tracked. Doing these activities at home, however, not only you, but anyone else sharing the domestic space, may be audible or visible to others. It's called "collateral capture." Children and pets often appear on-screen. A Canadian Member of Parliament was recently embarrassed on discovering he'd been seen naked on screen while changing after a jog.[5] Of course, those with digital assistants such as Amazon's Alexa don't really know what "she" "sees," either. But that is to focus only on video. All manner of data is now sucked out of homes, routinely, and by necessity, not mere convenience.

Let me stress that domestic surveillance is not new. Especially in richer countries, from nannycams to tracking devices for the elderly suffering from Alzheimer's, and from digital assistants such as Alexa to "smart" appliances such as Roomba vacuum cleaners, plenty of domestic surveillance occurred prior to the pandemic. Our focus here is its exponential expansion since the pandemic began. The level and range of domestic surveillance have been hugely augmented during the pandemic. Working remotely, from home, shopping online and learning online are just three dimensions of domestic targeting that are "re-scripting"[6] the privacy of the home in pandemic times.

Work "place" monitoring

Since the start of the pandemic, according to a Wirecutter report, the proportion of US managers using "bossware" systems for monitoring remote working has increased from 10 percent to more than 30 percent, and no doubt this will continue to rise the longer the pandemic lasts. This is over and above the "normal" use of software for electronically checking on employees, using well-known systems such as Slack, Google Workspace or Microsoft Teams. Again, even in non-pandemic times, some employers use third-party systems such as Prodoscore for the same purpose, because this "tracks the activities of each employee and calculates a productivity score based on their activity levels."[7]

A company called Sneek – why would anyone feel comfortable using anything from a company so named? – sells systems for watching employees at work. Sneek is a video-conferencing tool that is always on, by default. It takes a photo of employees through their webcam every 1–5 minutes – like a Zoom screen where no one is talking – intended, apparently, to "improve" office culture, but of course it is available to be checked by managers at any time. It's hard not to sympathize with someone who commented that it "made his skin crawl."[8]

Now, many people besides medical and public health personnel – such as warehouse workers – have been obliged to work in their regular work sites during the pandemic and some have also continued to work in hybrid circumstances, at home and in their customary premises. Yet others, such as those in delivery services, have spent increased time traveling for work and, in each case, most will have experienced intensified surveillance as employers try to keep track of the variety of "workplaces." Moreover, the varieties of surveillance have also increased to include health-related data-collection, as employers sign up as agents of public health authorities. They may require workers to use contact tracing apps, or to accept video and keyless entry for tracking, or to carry wearables.[9]

It must be stressed that workplace surveillance is nothing new.[10] Indeed, it is one of the most ancient forms of surveillance and was sharply accentuated by the development of capitalism. Karl Marx noted the crucial role of "overseers" in early capitalist workplaces.[11] Anyone who has ever had a job will be aware of the fact that their employer wishes to keep track of their activities. This can be done by many means. My students at the university, for instance, engage in a process of evaluating their courses, which includes comments on the performance of the professor – comments that are attached to reports from the Head of Department to the Dean, and that affect everything from "merit" salary increases to prospects for promotion. Professors themselves have to make their own annual report.

In this case, the surveillance is evidently known about by employees and there is a union agreement that, if done according to the rules, these procedures are acceptable. The massive rise of electronic monitoring methods from the end of the twentieth century allows for a wide range of software tools that are hidden, surreptitious and susceptible to abuse. Data may easily be gathered on employees; email and internet use are often monitored, tracking the whereabouts of employees; biometric measures and sometimes more covert forms of surveillance supplement or supplant more social kinds, such as I describe in my own case of self-policing and annual reporting. Of course, in a university that uses Microsoft 365, with Outlook for email and MS Teams for conferencing, opportunities do exist for more electronic monitoring.[12]

Prior to the pandemic, workplace surveillance was already changing its character as digital technologies offered new opportunities. Today's organizations are surveillant, argues management professor Kirstie Ball, and this can be by either social or technological means, or both. As she notes, "the nature and intensity of surveillance says much about how a company views its employees."[13] Intensified workplace surveillance has been normalized in many spheres. One area of increased surveillance is biometrics, in which data originating in the body may be recorded and measured, and the pandemic gives opportunities for this to expand. What happens in the physical workplace is one thing

– what happens in remote working conditions is clearly different.

To give an example from one country, the UK, in April 2020, 45 percent of those employed were working at least partially from home. And 86 percent of those were doing so because of COVID-19.[14] The chances of their being monitored remotely as well, are high, if only because the tools facilitating home-based work are digital, with surveillance capacities baked-in. In fact, many other systems suddenly found a ready market. After all, the shift from office and factory took place very rapidly, with no prior planning. And, as someone observed, "with more of their staffers spending the day in their pyjamas, employers have an increasingly difficult task when it comes to figuring out how hard employees are working."[15]

Around the world, the International Labour Association calculates that, even at the start of the pandemic, home-based work rose internationally from 7.9 percent in 2019 to between 13 and 15 percent in March 2020. These figures reflected similar ones in Brazil and Italy, while in India 90 percent of information technology workers (who number 4.3 million) shifted to full-time telework. This matches the situation in many countries where it is primarily professional and technical workers who can work from home.[16]

Work monitoring systems are widely used in commercial settings in many countries. In Europe and North America, these include CCTV, biometric identifiers, RFID (Radio Frequency Identification) and keystroke tracking. "OccupEye" was used at the *Telegraph* in the UK – a box under the desk tracking attendance and body temperature to gauge productivity.[17] Certain banks are known to use "Humanyze" badges that see and hear all their employees do, analyzing the speech volume as well as tracking where they go during the day, and with whom they meet. "Clickstream" collects specific data, reporting on how the computer and internet are used through the day. Some of these are used in the public sector – at least in Canada – as well.[18]

One particularly interesting finding of an empirical study of how workers respond to workplace surveillance is that they often rate visual surveillance – CCTV, photos, even Humanyze – as more intrusive than computer software – Clickstream, key-logging, internet analysis – which in fact amasses far more data. Such findings of worker perceptions may help to explain why there seems to be relatively little negative response to remote-working surveillance. Indeed, workers might wish to reassure their employers that they continue to be fully productive away from the office or factory.[19] Ironically, company expectations that workers will be more productive if they are surveilled may be disappointed. Researcher Claudia Pagliari observes that employees can be depressed – leading to lower productivity – by feeling that they are in a goldfish bowl.[20]

Things differ around the world, of course. In Japan, for instance, while many have been home-working during the pandemic, some would prefer to be back in the office, so that they *can* be seen while at work. One 32-year-old in a Tokyo publishing house said that he would prefer to be present in the office so that his boss will notice him, believing that the traditional workplace culture is hard to transfer online.[21] Many working from home in Japan discover that they are vulnerable to the flood of new means of monitoring such telework – something they have in common with others in many countries. After all, according to one estimate, the demand for employee monitoring tools rose by 108 percent by April 2020.[22] Popular products included Time Doctor, DeskTime and Kickidler.

There is little doubt, then, that monitoring work-at-home is becoming a major industry in its own right in the wake of the pandemic. This was, in a sense, predictable, but it raises multiple questions for the future, especially as many predict that home-working will persist after the pandemic is over. After all, companies can use funds saved on space for monitoring equipment, while employees have higher costs – for instance, of heating and cooling their homes.[23] Domestic targets of surveillance will continue to find that their employers have access to what happens in the home, in several simultaneous dimensions. Workers may be increasingly outsourced and monitored internationally, and the care burden of women will become heavier.[24]

School-at-home monitoring

Distance learning has been a feature of post-secondary education for many years – I myself was employed as a tutor for the UK's Open University in the mid-1980s – and it allows for those who might not otherwise be able to study at university to do so from home. In the 1980s, we used the familiar tools of the postal service, telephone, radio and television. The course I taught, "Information Technology (IT) and Society," was one of the world's first to use – and to study – IT, and we used very clunky "acoustic couplers" to enable short electronic messages to pass between professor and student. That course did include consideration of surveillance issues, but I do not recall anyone ever raising the question of whether learning from home could itself be considered as a surveillant activity.

Fast-forward 35 years and those involved in distance learning today are all too aware of the surveillant capacities in the panoply of proctoring, learning management and teleconferencing distance learning systems. Surveillance today is baked into these learning tools[25] and their soaring levels of use during the pandemic provide another way for surveillance to target the domestic sphere. They make the home more porous than ever to the scrutiny of others, reframing its privacy.[26] There is the straightforward sense in which the otherwise private rooms – often bedrooms – of university and college students are made public to others, including, most evidently, fellow-students and professors. This carries with it some obvious risks to visual as well as territorial privacy, as previously protected aspects of both students and spaces are opened to known and unknown others. And there is also the sense that the academic activities of students are exposed in new and sometimes unwelcome ways.

For the invigilation or proctoring of exams, for instance, students feel very uneasy as they are required to show their room for the camera's inspection to check that no prohibited materials are present, and then to allow the system – such as Examity – to monitor, or lock, their web browsers and keystrokes for the duration of the exam. One father heard from his son that he felt "creeped out" by the extent of exam monitoring by "Proctorio," another examination system. Apparently, some students who fail exams do so because the camera caught them "mouthing the questions or looking round their room while thinking, behaviour the system interprets as talking to someone off-screen."[27]

In the US, 54 per cent of universities use remote proctoring services, although, due to student pushback, 51 per cent say that privacy concerns do make them hesitate.[28] Dartmouth College, in New Hampshire, experienced unwanted controversy after several medical students were accused of cheating in exams, based on a flawed review of logs from an online learning tool, Canvas. Worse still, said the Electronic Frontier Foundation (EFF), "those attempting to assert their rights have been met by a university administration more willing to trust opaque investigations of opaque data sets rather than their own students."[29]

It seems to be a panic reaction that drives institutions of higher learning to adopt online surveillance methods for remote learning during a pandemic. Of course, cases exist of academic dishonesty, but have our deans and provosts considered the full range of issues raised? One has to do with the fact that students, like everyone else, are under stress during a persistent global pandemic. Surely, to increase the anxiety during an examination by using the crude instruments mentioned above will only exacerbate the general sense of stress. Another question relates to the organization of the exams themselves.

Might it not be possible, asks a physics professor from Carleton University, to randomize questions for large classes, rather than to use intrusive forms of monitoring?[30] Perhaps the pandemic could prompt questions about the usefulness of exams themselves?

A third query, equally serious, is about the ways in which online monitoring of students – particularly by requiring cameras to be left on during a teleconferencing class, may actually create situations where students feel threatened, or in which they are unequally treated along racial, gendered or class lines. To oblige students to expose their homes and private spaces – or even to maintain eye contact – may be at least culturally insensitive for some minority groups. Also, poorer students may not be able to maintain their online presence with the camera on due to low bandwidth. Being "camera-ready" is an expectation that may affect some women more than men, thus disadvantaging some along gender lines.[31]

While this discussion has focused mainly on post-secondary education, many high school students and younger have also had to learn from home during the pandemic. The issues facing them are similar to those in higher education and include "corporate tracking of students' activities inside and outside the classroom, discrimination against young people from marginalized communities … and the sale of student data to third parties," for advertising purposes.[32] Google is among the most popular purveyors of online teaching and learning tools in Western countries, but many argue – and even take legal action as a result – that this massive data-mining company monitors children using their technology without their knowledge or parental permission.[33]

Concerns are also apparent among Chinese parents of young children, who are no less dubious about schooling-at-home than those elsewhere. A 2020 survey showed that the vast majority of the sample (92.7 percent) had online learning experiences with their children, in sessions that were usually less than 30 minutes long. Parents noted many shortcomings of online learning, regretted their children's lack of capacity to maintain concentration, and felt inadequate to the task of being teaching assistants.[34] Nothing was mentioned in that context about which companies provided the software, what sorts of data they collect or how it is used. But then, there seems to be all too little awareness of these issues in Western societies either.

Among the cascading new challenges presented by home-based activities during the pandemic is the issue of how students are remotely monitored – and by whom, with what effects. As with the other issues mentioned above, there is both a question of distress within the period of COVID-19, and one of what will happen after the pandemic is officially over. Certainly, educational authorities at every level are challenged by rising costs – especially of university teachers – and have been searching for years for new ways of reducing such costs. Will the pandemic prompt a more decisive move towards remote learning, along with its accompanying modes of crude surveillance?

Online shopping from home

The pandemic provoked multiple remedies to the sudden shock of unavailable commodities and services. Even people who were concerned about data and privacy found themselves sacrificing their usual standards, succumbing to surveillance as an apparent necessity. As one digital privacy reporter confessed, "I gave away tons of personal data to get the things I needed. Food came from grocery and restaurant delivery services. Everything else – clothes, kitchen tools, vanity ring light for Zoom calls, office furniture – came from online shopping platforms."[35]

The pandemic prompted online shopping on an unprecedented scale. Consumers went online as stores were closed or only open at limited times. And they still had to make their transactions online to enable curbside pickup, where available. And, of course, they wished to avoid opportunities for infection. Even by April 2020, e-commerce package delivery had increased by more than 60 percent on the equivalent time in 2019. Postmates, Doordash and Instacart become household names overnight in the US.[36] In India, where many millions shop routinely at local, neighborhood, unorganized stores, online shopping became a regular alternative for many better-off Indians. They bought groceries, laptops and headphones for schooling and working from home, plus wellness items such as masks, sanitizers and fitness products.[37]

Among the many countries where online shopping has skyrocketed, some of the most affected are in emerging economies, according to an UNCTAD study.[38] The increase in online shopping is highest in countries such as China and Turkey; it rose far less in countries such as Germany or Switzerland, where e-commerce was already a popular practice. In Brazil, online consumption habits altered significantly, with a larger proportion buying essential items, including food, beverages and medicines. E-commerce grew by 65.8 percent in the first five months of the pandemic alone, including from smaller merchants and bricks-and-mortar stores.[39]

In China, during the first nine months of 2020, online shopping amounted to 24.3 percent of all sales. This rate continued, despite the decline of the COVID-19 pandemic in that country later in 2020. The chief beneficiaries were Meituan Dianping – China's biggest online delivery firm, by greatly increasing its food services – along with Alibaba and JD.com.[40] A key feature of Alibaba's success was the increase in its global market, especially in the area of PPE – Personal Protective Equipment. Spain, Italy and Pakistan benefitted from the increased availability of PPE, as countries hard-hit by the virus.[41]

Among the businesses to prosper, Amazon was the clear winner, around the world, from DC to Dublin to Delhi. By the end of July 2020, Amazon's profits were higher than any year of its 26 years in business, as their revenue jumped 40 percent. While others shed workers – Greyhound Canada, the bus company, closed down after nearly 100 years' service in May 2021, for instance – Amazon added 400,000 workers to its payroll in 2020, mainly in warehousing and delivery operations.[42] This mega-corporation gathers and analyzes detailed data from every one of its millions of customers, in order, in part, to nudge them into further purchases.

The name of Amazon is synonymous, for many, with its recommending technology. You buy one thing, and it suggests other similar items. This system works through "collaborative filtering" which is a process whereby the cluster of suggestions it makes to the consumer is created by building a profile of each customer. It compares that profile with other similar ones in its data system, and offers ideas on what that consumer could buy based on what other similar ones have purchased. Its US competitors include Walmart and Target, both also using the same kind of collaborative filtering, but they are seemingly unable to hold a candle to Amazon.

Amazon's primary business is extracting and processing data, which it does in order not just to sell products but also to develop relationships with customers. They both collect data on all their users, and also sell that data to third parties. As researcher Emily West notes, Amazon's trove of consumer data includes "purchases, product wish lists, page clicks, time spent on pages, searches, emails opened, and products reviewed and rated – to create predictive algorithms that can be used to make its products and services ever more irresistible to consumers."[43] But this seems much less spooky to consumers when Amazon's friendly assistant, "Alexa," who uses this data to provide customized services to users, also has access to their personal data, so that "she" can use such intimate surveillance as a welcome "service" to customers.

Even without Alexa's help, online platform companies still find ways around the "creep factor" associated with knowing that companies are tracking your moves. They offer incentives to pull people in, or make offers through their loyalty programs. Target Circle, for instance, offers a 1 percent discount on each purchase – redeemable on a future purchase – and a 5 percent birthday discount.[44] What they are unlikely to tell consumers, however, is that they may be profiled as "undesirable" customers, or that their systems are not fully secure.

Not all online shopping operates in this fashion during the COVID-19 crisis. Some – from the local farmers' market, for example – simply connects producers with consumers as a genuine service, during the pandemic and until the actual market can open for face-to-face business again. But the vast majority of online shopping, if not carried out in relation to Amazon, is offered by businesses that aspire to be like Amazon. This once again means that those companies are constantly learning more about what happens within the home and how best to position themselves to sell even more to those who inhabit those homes.

However, questions are definitely raised about online shopping and surveillance, especially in relation to the giant corporations such as Amazon. One wonders how much awareness really exists of the targeting involved in online shopping, or how that targeting depends on complex consumer profiles. In the US, awareness of targeting exists in a solid proportion – between a third and a half – of respondents in several studies. Once consumers are aware of targeting, they are far more wary about their involvement in online shopping – or at least this was the case in the US prior to the pandemic.

Negative opinions about targeting have the effect of reducing interest in making purchases.[45]

The increased levels of online shopping may well continue after the pandemic, which once more has implications not only for the datafied lives of those who so shop, but also for the environment, which is affected by the delivery trade, and of course for those without access to the means of shopping from home. And, during the pandemic, it is also worth remembering that if we do shop in person, we're more or less required to use credit or debit cards as a matter of pandemic hygiene, and more consumer data flows again. This is a critically important area for analysis and policy, not only during, but also after, COVID-19.

Where from here?

Pandemic surveillance is clearly not all about contact tracing and public health data systems. It cannot but include many other areas of enlarged surveillance activities, not least those that now extend far more deeply into the domestic sphere. This means that such surveillance touches on the lives of people of all ages, from the elderly to the young, from men to women, and from the relatively well-off to the perennially poor.

Situations seen in this chapter have mainly been marked by their association with relatively well-off populations in the so-called global north. The surveillance is no less real and problematic, of course, but what we have discussed is thus limited to specific kinds of issues. Parallel problems also exist, for instance, in the surveillance of gig workers who have been supplying homes, in both the global north and the global south. Also, the relationship between "Zoom fatigue"[46] and surveillance is unexplored, along with fuller consideration of the ties and tugs between remote and domestic work. Many lives have been made more precarious by the pandemic and this is not unconnected, in many cases, with the monitoring of domestic activities, especially work.

Precarious lives exist in every society, and the conditions producing them are similar across the world, especially in situations where surveillance capitalism is making rapid inroads. This "mode of prediction," as I think of it, is by definition dependent on data and on the tools used to analyze and use data – something we explore further in the following chapters. But precarious lives are visible in the clearest profile – double-entendre intended – in countries of the global south.

Writing on Chile, Claudio Celis Bueno sees this with great clarity. Work overload is routine, and exacerbated by the use of digital technologies. And if people are working, learning, shopping and living at home, then this fact further blurs the distinctions between work and non-work time. And digital technologies, with their intrinsic capacities for ongoing surveillance, contribute to the process. Things get worse when one also considers relations between women and men in the home. In Chile, for instance, a survey shows that 92 percent of women believe that there is "inequality in the distribution of household tasks and in the care of children," which negatively impacts their capacity to work remotely.[47]

The pandemic prompted a proliferation of domestically

targeted surveillance. Individuals were trapped indoors, under constant "inspection," as Foucault commented. But while the "roll calls" and "visits" of "syndics"[48] described in the seventeenth-century plague town were in person, at the door, today's are remote and freely enter the home. In the following chapter, we explore further the contribution of these digital technologies – all of which are surveillant – to social disadvantage and data injustice. Such technologies are not inevitably negative in their social impact, but the way in which they have been designed, developed and deployed makes them so.

4
Data Sees All?

Data can be very useful, during a pandemic crisis, as at other times. It is vital for understanding some situations, crafting responses, allocating resources and evaluating the effectiveness of policies. However, as three highly competent data researchers show, "incomplete or incorrect data can also muddy the waters, obscuring important nuances within communities, ignoring important factors such as socioeconomic realities and creating a false sense of panic or safety, not to mention other harms such as needlessly exposing private information. Right now, bad data could produce serious missteps with consequences for millions."[1]

To live through the pandemic is to be inundated with data. COVID-19 hit in an era when data has become central to almost every facet of contemporary life. Unsurprising, then, that data was seized as a contributory way of dealing with the pandemic. Every day we wake to fresh statistics, data about the course of the contagion, visualizations of the virus, predictions of its progress. Every newscast, every newsfeed, every public health official tells us what the data discloses. This includes responses to data: April 8, 2020 stands out in the US as the day when the most widely asked question was "how to make a face mask with fabric?"[2] Data, it seems, sees all.

Except that it doesn't. Data can only tell the story from a particular vantage point, depending on the reliability of the original sources, the curation of the data, the algorithms used to analyze it, its interpretation and use. Data does not speak for itself; it has to be interpreted, packaged for consumption.[3] Data does not see the whole scene; it paints only a partial picture. And it doesn't necessarily see accurately, with 20-20 vision. It may show some significant details, such as modeling the likely rise of COVID-19 cases, but miss others that are vitally important. This chapter takes us behind the scenes – that are sometimes quite badly lit, to say the least – to try to understand pandemic surveillance in the mysterious world of data.

The word "surveillance" once referred to literal seeing, as in watching-over, which is what the original French means. The secret agent, for example, is tasked with surreptitiously following the suspect – keeping the target in sight without being seen. Even the CCTV camera, when first invented, depended on a control room of watchers who were required to scrutinize those screens for signs of trouble.[4] In these cases, the seeing is directly visual, though still always mediated.[5] But, today, surveillance seldom requires literal sight or actual watching. Today, it is more often data that makes us visible to others, most frequently through the use of smartphones. This is the data by which we are represented, and data that leads to our being treated one way or another.

The 2020 onset of the pandemic prompted an urgent and massive search for the means of diagnosing COVID-19, including both conventional testing and also the use of the latest AI and Machine Learning techniques. Rather like the 9/11 moment, when the attacks on New York and Washington sparked an explosion of high-tech "solutions" to terrorism, COVID-19 has led to many digital proposals, and in particular attracted thousands of eager enthusiasts for Machine Learning and AI to apply their skills to finding Big Data diagnostic tools to address the COVID-19 crisis.

Starting in mid-2020, and persisting through 2021 to an undefined future, research teams around the world formed to find ways of harnessing data for everything from modeling the pandemic pathways to improving the speed and accuracy of diagnosis. While the modeling is clearly surveillant, the diagnostic challenge showed very clearly the importance of appropriate data handling. At the same time, as we saw in chapter 3, many other companies were eagerly producing and promoting surveillance systems to support the migration of office, store and school to the home, where data also resides, to be gathered and mined for profit.

This chapter begins with a cautionary tale. The intention is not to cast doubt on all efforts to use data in the attempt to contain the contagion – many, as I have already stressed, are valuable and are already saving lives. Rather, caution is called for because leading researchers in the field have also expressed concerns about pandemic data-handling, and their worries indicate that serious problems do have to be faced in this area.

Following this particular case-study, we shall look together at some of the ways in which assumptions about data are being questioned by scholars of many stripes, also with a view to trying to improve the relevance and fitness-for-purpose of some technical tools. Lastly, we shall explore some key elements of approaches to "data justice" that might help such data techniques to be fully effective, in the sense of being fair to those whose data is used, and for whom the data will be beneficial.

A cautionary tale about data-handling

Much enthusiasm was expressed, during the COVID-19 pandemic, about the potential help available not only from data analysis in general, but from Machine Learning and Artificial Intelligence (AI) in particular. Keeping things simple, Margaret Boden, a leading exponent, says that AI "seeks to make computers do the sorts of things that minds can do."[6] For example, AI is in a hybrid car that we just bought. The first time we drove at night, we suddenly realized that the headlights dipped when oncoming cars appeared and then returned to full beam. Machine Learning (ML) adds probability theory and statistics and is used especially for data mining, and for processing Big Data. On a small scale, our new car also "learns" each of our driving styles. Should we be reassured or disturbed?

For detecting and prognosticating the presence of COVID-19 in a patient, ML shows much promise in the case of chest radiographs and "CAT" scans. So, there was a rush of articles describing how ML could assist in these much-needed tasks and arguing for their clinical utility. But many results were deemed by experts to be unsatisfactory. In March 2021, a major investigation by scientists at Cambridge and Manchester Universities in the UK concluded that "none of the models identified are of potential clinical use due to their methodological flaws and/or underlying biases."[7]

As one of its senior authors, James Rudd, from the University of Cambridge Medical School, commented in an interview, "The international machine learning community went to enormous efforts to tackle the COVID-19 pandemic using machine learning." But he went on to say that, while the early studies were promising, their methods and reporting were flawed. This meant that the results were just not up to par – neither fully reliable nor reproducible in ways that would make them useful in the doctor's office or hospital.

Among the deficiencies is what the authors refer to as "Frankenstein datasets." The original monster of Mary Shelley's imagination was gruesomely constructed from cadavers collected by the student, Frankenstein, who promptly abandoned his "hideous progeny" in horror. The datasets named after this student are made with duplicate images obtained from other datasets. The latter were also found to have a frequently encountered problem, which was that they too were already composites. All this, along with the very name, sparks a spine-shiver. But only one in five COVID-19 diagnosis or prognosis models shared their algorithm – computer code – so others could reproduce results claimed in literature. Such sharing is basic to good practice, especially in the context of a global pandemic, where experts in other countries are struggling with the same problems, albeit on a different scale.

According to this critical study, there are also strict limits on the usefulness of the algorithms used, particularly if the data relates only to specific segments of the population. Lead author Michael Roberts comments that "any machine learning algorithm is only as good as the data it's trained on ... Especially for a brand-new disease like COVID-19, it's vital that the training data is as diverse as possible because, as we've seen throughout this pandemic, there are many different factors that affect what the disease looks like and how it behaves."[8]

This cautionary tale offers a glimpse into what might happen as a result of hasty research, and a good dose of data*ism* – overweening belief in the efficacy of data. The flaws and biases of the Machine Learning-based diagnostic tools produce what the authors refer to, several times, as "highly optimistic reported performance." The questions of how data is collected and curated, analyzed and used, are major ones, and this chapter looks into some of the key issues raised by Big Data, Machine Learning and Artificial Intelligence in the world of pandemic surveillance at large.

Data Sees All?

Dubious assumptions about data

In the twenty-first century, declares John Cheney-Lippold, "we are data."[9] In other words, for practical purposes, data relating to us is collected, analyzed and used to indicate "who we are" to companies, government departments, schools, the police and others. What counts, to them, is not so much how we might identify ourselves to them, but what they know of our "data-double."[10] It is tremendously important to recognize this, because in ordinary, daily life we think of ourselves quite differently, in terms of the roles we perform, or what we call our "identity." But our data-double can easily constrain those roles or give a different sense of who we are than what we'd like to project.

This is because our "digital" world is a data-dependent domain, a world that has been *datafied*. The idea of datafication is commonplace, today, but often glossed as an unquestionable good. José van Dijck prods the idea, exposing its soft underbelly of dubious claims about being and knowing. In particular, she uses the incisive term "data*ism*," to indicate a "*belief* in the objective quantification and potential tracking of all kinds of human behaviour."[11] Dataism also assumes that those collecting and analyzing data can be trusted to collect, interpret and share this data. Such *belief* and *trust* are highly relevant in a world where surveillance using copious quantities of data is a constant process. And this is not just by police, security authorities or public health agencies, but also by the platforms that now play a prominent role in everyday life and whose popular use is currently accentuated by the pandemic.

In the Netherlands, José van Dijck and Donya Alinejad argue, questions of belief and trust have become even more significant during the pandemic. They argue that this is because of the expansion of social media as a means of disseminating health-related information, and the difficulty of distinguishing between institutional and networked information sources.[12] Social media is a two-edged sword of science communication, observe van Dijck and Alinejad, and can be used both to undermine and to enhance health information sharing. After all, social media is in the marketplace of ideas and thus pursues profit, which may or may not aid the common good. And this argument applies equally to the question of surveillance. How far should social media surveillors – that collect and process more data than anyone – be trusted to do the right thing with that sensitive data?

Very early in the pandemic, data expert Rob Kitchin could already see where things were heading. He warned that public health data would quickly become a minefield. Worried about the rushed rollout of so many surveillance tools – apps, thermal cameras, biometric wearables and predictive biometrics for contact tracing, quarantine control, travel, distancing and symptom tracking – he questioned both their practical efficacy and also their implications for civil liberties as well as for public health.[13] In Italy, for instance, the very hard-hit region of Lombardy used thermal cameras on drones to warn – using loudspeakers – those apparently breaking regulations by being in a prohibited area during curfew.[14] But both the accuracy of the readings varies and the lack of consent raises legal issues, despite the police claim that they were granted special powers.

Some of these issues were teased out in chapter 2, especially in relation to contact tracing apps. But the list of issues arising from the use of surveillance technologies in the pandemic is long, including: technological solutionism; robust, domain-informed design; pilot-testing and quality assurance; fitness-for-purpose; potentially fragmented data sources; data coverage and resolution; data quality; reliability; and false negatives/ positives. Many are directly related to data. And, as Kitchin foresaw, the utility of many of such data-based solutions was oversold, including some Public Health Intelligence tools.

The science of Public Health Intelligence (PHI) is crucial to the pandemic, to discover what is happening and what *will happen*.[15] On a very large scale, the WHO runs a "global alert and response" that systematically gathers official reports and rumors of suspected outbreaks from a wide range of formal and informal sources.[16] The formal sources are public health departments around the world, while the informal ones include electronic media and online discussion groups. The aim of such PHI is to detect public health "events" as they unfold, or even *before* they happen. However, it is very important that the informal sources are not seen as superior to the conventional formal ones.

Back in 2008, Google made some bold predictions about flu outbreaks, claiming that they could outdo the US Centers for Disease Control (CDC) in showing where and when influenza would peak. The idea was disarmingly simple. Google has access to millions of searches and when people start to search for symptoms or ways of dealing with flu, the volume and type of those searches could be tracked in order to calculate where outbreaks were occurring. Combine this with flu tracking information from the CDC and Google could accurately estimate flu prevalence two weeks before the CDC.[17]

"Google Flu Trends" ran for several years, until it failed spectacularly to predict the 2013 peak of the flu season by 140 percent. An article in *Science* in 2014[18] concluded that the errors were related to the assumption that Google's methods were *better* than traditional ones, and could supplant them. This in turn related to "Big Data hubris" and "algorithm dynamics." The former is already hinted at – the problem lay in an over-reliance on Google data. The latter, algorithm dynamics, is what engineers do to improve the commercial service, as well as what is done by consumers using the service. So consumer panic could have skewed the figures but, more likely, the culprit was consumer confusion about the difference between cold and flu symptoms, say the authors. By trying to improve service to customers, Google ended up generating data differently. Several lessons are suggested for improving potential findings; checking the algorithm is one, and another is not assuming that the simple *size* of "Big Data" is sufficient to ensure success.

We turn now to a specific question: How does data affect ordinary people in everyday life? This is critically important, and leads into two major issues to be taken up in chapters 5 – how data discrimination operates in the pandemic – and 6 – how data relates to government and corporate power. We start with the question of how surveillance data makes people visible, as potential or actual COVID-19 victims, as well as in other ways.

We then go on to show how they are represented by the data – where, in particular, "race" may be an issue. And, lastly, we ask how people are treated on the basis of those representations. In each case, it is also possible to see how data used for non-medical or non-health reasons, in pandemic surveillance, are also affected by the same problems – how people are made visible, represented and treated by data collection, analysis and use. The use of data has become a central issue in matters of health – as in other areas – affecting, especially, issues of freedom and fairness.

Data makes people visible

Though many surveillors – especially platform companies – are not very transparent about what exactly they are doing, they make our lives very transparent to them. It is simply impossible for ordinary citizens to keep up with what data is being collected on them, especially with so many other pandemic preoccupations to deal with. Both the data for contact tracing and that for vaccine passes make people visible, and so, of course, do those kinds of para-pandemic surveillance examined in chapter 2.

In the former, one's status in relation to COVID-19 infection is made visible; in the latter, it is the matter of certifying vaccination. In the world of domestic targeting, data reveals to employers how employees are working remotely; to educational institutions how students are performing, especially in exams; and to online shopping platforms, what consumers are buying and how that relates to their profiles, rank and status. This varies in different countries and regions, and thus in the details of causes and consequences, but the basic process of surveillance making people visible occurs everywhere.[19]

Thus, data is universally used as a "way of seeing," of making us visible to others. And those others are institutions, authorities and companies that represent power. Understandably, public health officials wish to know who has been with whom, where and for how long, and the data they collect and analyze allows them to "see" the lives of those within each category set up to distinguish those requiring further observation or treatment. Likewise, if people wish to travel and not to remain restricted by the stay-at-home lockdowns of the pandemic, they may have to carry some proof of vaccination that marks them as at less risk than others of spreading the virus.

However, in the UK, for example, the Equalities and Human Rights Commission (EHRC) warned that being obliged to carry a COVID-status certificate could amount to unlawful indirect discrimination. In twentieth-century South Africa under Apartheid, "pass books" were used to distinguish between "blacks" and others. A COVID-status certificate could easily produce a similar two-tier society, they argued, based on the visibility produced by the data. While it could be a proportionate means of easing restrictions, it could further exclude groups whose take-up rate is lower – including migrants, those from ethnic minority backgrounds, and lower socio-economic groups. The ways they are made visible would have an impact on the lives of such groups. The prime minister suggested that the documents could be required for entry into pubs or theatres.[20]

Much hangs, then, on how visible or invisible one is, in many different contexts. Again, the arguments for the surveillance are clear enough. The contact tracing app is intended to reduce levels of infection, to ensure that hospitals are able to cope with the pressure of patients needing care and, ultimately, to save lives. Similarly, the vaccine passes are supposed to allow for parts of the economy to reopen and for people to travel more freely – say, to see family and friends from whom they have been cut off for many months. While one might question aspects of these aspirations – for instance, an unfortunate utilitarianism lies behind some arguments, a matter to which reference has already been made – there are clearly some legitimate needs to which apps or certificates offer a resolution.

In the case of our relationships at work, school, in healthcare or commerce, the process of being made visible is more opaque. Offices and factories have surveillance systems but they are rapidly being augmented for remote working, and the capacities of the surveillance are not always clear. Who guessed that "bossware" would enable managers to see employees literally as well as digitally, for instance? Students have been aware for years of the "learning platforms" that allow professors to follow their progress online, checking things such as which readings have been consulted, but the pandemic prompted a ramping-up of such monitoring, for remote participation. And, as we have seen, we all contribute to surveillance by accidentally making ourselves visible – with every click, sometimes every eye movement – to platform companies such as Amazon or Alibaba, who sell our data to other companies: data that can also make its way into government agencies or political parties.

Dealing with these issues is difficult because responses to them have traditionally been couched in the language of individual rights, such as privacy. Any abuses have to be clearly seen so that affected individuals can name them and seek redress. But, as Taylor notes, "This is rendered problematic by the invisible ... nature of 'seeing' through data technologies, but also by the fact that many of the negative impacts of data occur on the group as much as the individual level."[21]

Data represents people in particular ways

It is not merely that surveillance data makes people visible, however. It also represents them – or fails to represent them – in specific ways. For instance, as many have noted, not everyone, by any means, has a smartphone. This means that, as contact tracing apps require a smartphone, and if they really work to alert people to the possibility of infection, not to have a phone is to be data-less, in this context, and thus potentially vulnerable to needless infection. And, as we saw in chapter 2, there are many ways in which contact tracing apps easily offer false positives and false negatives, so that, when they are in use, they are also prone to misrepresent those who appear in the system.

Or if, as in the Philippines, errors and discrepancies in anonymized COVID-19 data produced a drop in publicly reported cases of infection, this clearly puts many more at risk. As a Philippine senator commented, "garbage data" could produce "garbage decisions" by the government.[22] Such "garbage data" has negative effects, again, because of how people are represented by the data.

Linnet Taylor, whose scheme we are following – loosely – here, uses the example of Aadhaar, the registration and identification system used in India, to show how the poor in particular may be grossly under-represented, a process that has been magnified during COVID-19. The system completely misses the materiality of poverty – meaning, for example, fingerprints cannot even be gathered from those whose fingers have become worn through a lifetime of hard toil, and the iris scans of the elderly are unusable due to malnutrition.

Her other example, in this context, is the proposal by a consulting company, working with the European Space Agency, to monitor the progress of migrants traveling toward the southern borders of the European Union. The plan was to watch groups congregating on beaches, monitoring things like their social media posts to predict who was heading for specific destinations, and who would cross when. They would then sell the data to border enforcement and migration authorities, so that they could be algorithmically sorted prior to arrival, according to their "desirability." From those calculations, those authorities could pre-sort their chances of obtaining asylum.[23] Migrants, too, are especially at risk during the pandemic.[24]

But how people are represented by data is not a simple matter. For the data is also processed through algorithms, the codes that are used to translate the basic information into more usable forms for specific purposes. Such algorithms are the crucial determinants, within each system, of how people are represented. And a basic obstacle to our understanding of this is that algorithms, as Frank Pasquale observes so eloquently, create a *Black Box Society*.[25] They just can't be "seen."

Algorithms are not just "technical" and "neutral." They are powerful means of organizing data for particular purposes. Black boxes are found in planes and other transportation, to record technical data, but the image also suggests the obscurity to most people of data-processing. The black box *society* is a sorting machine for handling massive amounts of data about people's daily lives, behavior and movement – including health data. In the case of COVID-19, where the use of self-learning algorithms has been accelerated, they have been shown to create a feedback loop. A 21-country study[26] indicates how the algorithms turn the "raw"[27] data into policy recommendations, which are then adopted by administrators. This then affects the data, which in turn finds its way back into the self-learning algorithms.

This has political consequences, affecting the democratic process, that are explored further in chapter 6. Decisions made by authorities are underpinned by the sorted data, which simplifies and thus distorts our understanding of what is actually happening. But this remains unquestioned by many, due to the complexity and opacity of the algorithms. The resulting policy discussions and even legal regulations may be determined from data that supposedly "sees all," but in fact offers a very blurry vision.

The idea that societies are unequal – that some are privileged, and others disadvantaged – is a truism. But many insist that the use of digital technologies and data practices – such as, in particular, algorithmic sorting – actually serve to deepen disadvantage and to perpetuate privilege. Indeed, Mirca Madianou describes this as a "second-order disaster" during the pandemic.[28] Among the social, political, economic, environmental and cultural factors that determine the course of the pandemic – beyond the pathogen itself – digital technology plays a significant role. There are many aspects of this, she argues, but a key one is dependence on "automation and algorithmic filtering" – something also argued, passionately, by Ruha Benjamin in her book on *Race after Technology*.[29]

Part of the problem is basic assumptions that can be baked into the system, such as that there is a "standard human" out there somewhere. As Stefania Milan points out, the standard human measure does not account for those treated as "others," or for the basic understanding that inequalities exist in every society.[30] But much Big Data rhetoric exudes notions like objectivity, rationality and certainty. It often has little time to discuss the ways in which data arrives in fits and starts, unevenly distributed and from sources of quite different levels of reliability, and tending to create feedback loops. It may also depend on mistaken notions like the "standard human."

As Linnet Taylor stresses, the data available on the spread of the disease is in part a product of how far public health authorities can capture and measure COVID-19's effects by the traces it leaves behind.[31] Some data, as we have seen, may be unavailable, or invisible, or will reflect the ways in which it was collected, analyzed or presented.

In the next chapter, more illustrations of the role of algorithmic sorting will be given, but it is worth emphasizing that this is a basic problem. It almost inevitably leads to people being treated in different ways, which skew basic fairness. As Norma Möllers argues, "The 'what most people do' style of making algorithms *always* privileges majorities and their perspectives and ignores and/or penalizes minorities and their perspectives." However democratic one's ideals of protecting minority rights, an "unresolvable tension" arises when the algorithms are made in ways where their "objectivity" is assumed.[32] No wonder Safiya Noble speaks of the emergence of "algorithms of oppression."[33] This tension has to be faced, because data also helps to determine how people are treated.

Data helps to determine how people are treated

Unfortunately, but not surprisingly, data also contributes to what might be termed "data-driven injustice" or algorithmic unfairness. Those ways in which people are represented by algorithms, often based

90

on a "standard human" view, eventuate in the ways that people are actually treated in particular ways, following the analysis. In China, if your color-coded health rating obliges you to stay home, facial recognition camera surveillance or drones outside your apartment window make you even more visible to the public health authorities. In this case, as in some other countries, the state limits citizen freedoms according to the classification received.

Just to take one example from the education field, Alivardi Khan experienced great difficulty trying to get the ExamSoft facial recognition system to recognize him as he took his New York State Bar exam. He tried sitting in front of a window at home where sunlight flooded in, and even set himself up in a bright bathroom with light shining off white tiles. Even when set up with a college room in which to write the exam, he had to wave his arms to prevent the automatic space lighting from switching off, thus further risking suspicion of exam-room misbehavior.[34] But the problem is that the algorithms are often constructed in ways that favor certain racial characteristics and not others, and engineers may be influenced by their own "race."[35] The algorithms affect how people are represented, and thus how they are treated.

Now, despite the difficulties, these systems cannot be dismantled easily, for many reasons. But, as awareness grows that data injustice may be a key component of today's pandemic – and other – data systems, so alternatives may be sought. This is a topic for the final chapter. But, for the present, despite the difficulties, some – such as Wim Naudé[36] – argue that the inadequate systems still produce some benefits, even if they are flawed. Some in the medical science data-systems field do recognize many serious shortcomings of present arrangements, arguing for massive reorganization, particularly of global public health databases.[37] And, as Taylor says, the real need is for a radically different way of governing data, but this has to be worked out in relation to already-existing systems and to an elevation of data justice to a place where it is recognized as a critical component of computer science, software engineering, AI and ML.

Another issue concerns what sorts of bodies are handling the data, especially in a surveillance capitalism context, which also affects their quality. In Canada, as in many countries, "virtual care" services are growing, prompted particularly by the pandemic. For instance, a grocery chain, Loblaw, has invested in a telemedicine company, and a telecom, Telus, in an electronic medical record company and a virtual care platform. Partnerships with pharmaceutical companies are sought after and emerging rapidly. They can advertise directly to healthcare providers, which leads to less appropriate and more expensive medications being prescribed.[38]

Physician-researchers Sheryl Spithoff and Tara Kiran, who provide this example, go on to show how, when health data is treated as a financial asset, patient health easily becomes secondary. Databases containing de-identified primary-care records are extremely valuable – at around 35–330 Canadian dollars each, according to one company. So, in addition to the issues with invisible algorithms, the context within which algorithms are developed makes a difference to outcomes as well. How people are treated, as well as made visible and represented, is the product of many significant factors.

The critical issue is *how* data is used. The apps, devices and platforms make a difference, of course, but the use of data to make visible, represent and treat people is the underlying process to be highlighted and confronted. How, in everyday life, people respond will also be significant. A constant theme in sociology is how, once described, categorized and analyzed, people respond to those descriptions, categories and analyses. And how this might make a difference to the ongoing accuracy of the original data.

Let's return to those "Frankenstein datasets" mentioned in the earlier example of the pitfalls of Machine Learning. The problem originated in dataism that places much more faith than is warranted in the possibilities of technology. This, alongside the rollout rush, helps to account for the ways in which dataism infuses so many well-meaning projects developed in 2020 and 2021. But its consequences – seen here in the ways that data makes people visible, represents them and treats them – can be dire.

Surveillance based on Big Data analytics as currently practiced is a way of reinforcing inequalities that are further explored in the next chapter. The shift toward corporate medical data platforms creates further problems, as does the haste with which many public health authorities, pressed to perform by governments wishing to demonstrate their decisive action, attempted to do so in ways that would also draw attention to their reliance on the latest data-handling methods.

We explore the consequences of data in the next two

chapters. But, as the quick fix was the problem in the first place, there's no such "fix" that will work for the pandemic problem, or for what will grow out of current developments. In the final chapter, we return to this, to propose that the basic cultural-philosophical problem lies in imagining that humans can transcend their limits, using technology.[39] If hubris is a basic challenge here, then the lasting "solution" to Frankenstein datasets and the rest must surely lie in a new-found humility.

5

Disadvantage and the Triage

Asli Farah caught COVID-19 from a co-worker with whom she carpooled to her job at an Edmonton, Canada, warehouse.[1] Health authorities sent her for testing, and she had no choice but to travel on two buses to get to her appointment. Isolated at home, feeling like she was in jail, she developed a tooth infection but was not able to get treatment. Asli recently immigrated to Canada and faced the additional challenge of a language barrier. Like many other members of minority groups around the world, black Canadians experience the negative effects of the pandemic disproportionately compared with majority groups.[2] They are more likely to report symptoms, to seek treatment, and are three times more likely to know someone who has died of the virus.[3]

But, deplorable as this is, it is not the whole story. Surveillance of various kinds, and in different ways, often serves to make things worse for already vulnerable groups in society. They may be made visible, represented and treated inappropriately within systems such as contact tracing apps. But this can also lead to other kinds of disadvantage, as marginalized groups are affected by disproportionate profiling, policing[4] and criminalization.[5] UNESCO recognizes this, warning that, during pandemics, "vulnerable people become even more vulnerable."[6] Near the start of the pandemic, Ruha Benjamin was already speaking about the gross differences in how black Americans were viewed and described in the context of COVID-19, drawing on classically mistaken notions such as "culture of poverty" that basically blame black people for their greater likelihood of contracting the virus.[7]

For several decades, surveillance has been considered by some scholars, policy makers and activists as a means of "social sorting."[8] That is to say, because the purpose of the surveillance is to find out about populations, the way of characterizing them is to categorize. That is, to divide populations into different groups for classification, so that the groups can be treated differently. This applies to police surveillance, trying to narrow down to suspects; workplace surveillance, to discover who is working most effectively; or consumer surveillance, to target the most likely customers with ads for the latest service or product. Hardly surprising, then, that the process of social sorting also occurs in relation to the largest digital surveillance surge ever, triggered by the COVID-19 pandemic.

Let's turn things around for a moment, to consider the sorting that happens in any hospital, which will help us to see how this works. In non-pandemic times, as now, when you go to the emergency department, you have to go through a "triage" process. The nurse on duty must sort out which patients are in most urgent need of attention and care. Surveillance-in-general works like this – it sorts between different categories in the population so that each group can receive treatment appropriate to their condition.

I was grateful for just this some years ago, trying to answer triage questions while in agony after a winter running accident – slipping on hidden ice – that caused a spiral fracture in my lower leg. The triage process works best – meaning *fairly* – when everyone knows the criteria by which decisions are made. It can work very *unfairly* – as when, for instance indigenous people in Australia or Canada[9] are assumed to have alcohol-related problems rather than serious illness. In the majority of cases in today's pandemic world, however, it is algorithms that hide, or at least obscure, those criteria.

COVID-19 has not only exposed how some populations are more vulnerable than others, and that there are inequalities of access to testing, appropriate hospital care, and vaccines. Pandemic surveillance also leads to variable treatment, such that some already marginalized groups experience negative discrimination. This is a systemic situation, albeit varying by country and region. And it is also a global issue of structural inequality and violence, along with neocolonialism and disposability. Situational awareness is a vital dimension of such attempts to discover what is really happening in a given context.

Poverty, marginalization and invisibility each tend to be penalized by the pandemic. Minority groups and those in poverty are likely to be worst affected. This may happen in one of two ways. On one hand, digital surveillance may be developed in ways that benefit only some citizens, not others. As we have seen, the most obvious case is the contact tracing apps, which by definition can only be useful – assuming they are successful – to those who have smartphones new enough to take advantage of the app. Those without up-to-date smartphones are likely to be among the poorer and more disadvantaged, but this group might also include those who have no wish to own a smartphone, for whatever reason.

On the other hand, the contact tracing systems may themselves contain biases. Their algorithms may affect a disproportionate number of people in certain population categories, depending on income, gender, caste, class or race, ethnicity and place of origin. But this is not only an effect of contact tracing apps; the very design of healthcare systems developed for dealing with the pandemic may itself reproduce or deepen already existing disadvantage. David Leslie, a researcher at the UK's Turing Institute, asks, "Does 'AI' stand for augmenting inequality in the era of COVID-19 healthcare?" Leslie pays particular attention to algorithmic bias in answering the question.[10] This is clearly depicted in figure 1.

As we have seen in other contexts, the inequalities relating to health surveillance may be associated with very straightforward factors such as the lack of a smartphone in some sectors of a given society. This is true of China, for example, where it is calculated that more than 250 million elderly people do not use such things. Recall that the Health Code contact tracing system,

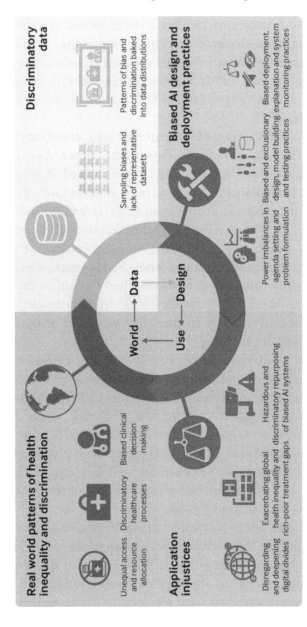

Figure 1. Reproduced with permission from David Leslie, and the *BMJ*, April 2021.

required for access to public transport as well as to most public places, depends upon smartphone use. A video circulated in China in 2020, showing a senior citizen "losing his cool" in frustration at his inability to gain access at a subway station in Dalian, in the province of Liaoning.[11]

And not all aspects of unequal consequences of surveillance have directly digital dimensions, either. Again in China, more traditional forms of government administrative surveillance continue to play an important role in unequal outcomes. People from COVID-19 "hotspots" Hubei and Wuhan have found themselves discriminated against in job applications, for example, because of the fear of contagion. A young man, Ye Xiaotian, cleared by a virus test, was interviewed for a position in an internet technology company in the southern city of Xiamen only to be told that they were not accepting applicants from Hubei.[12]

Such traditional forms of surveillance, carried out by workplaces and "community managers," may even cross international borders. China's COVID-Contain program stretched to Kingston, Ontario, when the parents of a graduate student visited in 2020 to greet a new grandson. Their workplaces and community trackers frequently checked how much longer they would be away and asked what their date of return was and for their travel schedule.

The rest of this chapter examines these issues, as they affect COVID-19 healthcare around the world and in a range of different ways. We begin with questions relating directly to the pandemic and public health surveillance and how – for instance, in China and India

– the required contact tracing apps depend on coded systems that reveal risk profiles of citizens. But there are also indirect ways in which non-health surveillance may intensify the disadvantage experienced by certain groups, such as prisoners.

Equally, others experience inequality through the *lack* of certain kinds of surveillance, or through their involvement in apparently unrelated "surveillance capitalism." Following this, the lens widens to examine how other kinds of surveillance also affect inequality and social disadvantage, especially along racial and socio-economic class lines. This points forward to the final chapter where, among other things, we call for an equity-focused global health agenda.

Pandemic disadvantage and healthcare surveillance

That the pandemic has revealed many kinds of social inequality is well known, and has prompted heart-searching about the hidden unfairness of many "normal" conditions preceding the pandemic, around the world. However, pandemic-related surveillance is also impli-cated in this, both by *what* it fails to reveal about the uneven social distribution of the pandemic *and* the ways in which surveillance is skewed to produce positively unfair social outcomes. Some of these effects are direct ones, such as those seen in the Chinese Health Code and the Indian Aarogya Setu apps. Others are indirect.

Now, the COVID-19 pandemic is a tragically appalling development, produced by a globalized world, and at the time of writing it has, of course, caused almost 3.5

million deaths – many suggest that this figure is lower than the *actual* figure – worldwide, as well as destroying development and deepening disadvantage. The mortality rates for India finally surpassed the ghastly figures for the USA (with its vastly smaller population)[13] in March 2021, so the drive to find ways to slow the spread of infection is fully understandable, and commendable as a top priority. However, it is also the case that good health is not the only priority for human flourishing. To be fair and appropriate, good health must be sought for *all*. The ways in which it is sought also affect outcomes, which can be very different for different social groups. Historical discrimination can easily be reinforced.[14]

Part of the difficulty, as we have seen, is that the use of, and assumptions about, the data can produce problems. Many governments around the world have been working hard to produce population-level data and to work out policies in relation to that. Ordinary citizens seldom hear about the difficulties attending data analysis, but they definitely exist and are not necessarily treated the same way in all countries. As Linnet Taylor says, "COVID-19, like all crises ... burrows into the faultlines of inequality, neglect and marginalization; it exposes the under-funding of essential services and the lack of attention to known risks."[15]

There are perceived risks, such as the level of trans-missibility of the virus, but also actual risks, to this or that particular person or group, that depend heavily on socio-economic factors, on geographical location and, indeed, on racialized distinctions. For instance, the Indian government blamed the Muslim community for the spread of the virus, after a Tabighli Jamaat event in New Delhi in March 2020 that attracted outsiders. But it seems that the combination of what one expert described as "sampling errors" – from over-testing this group compared to others – and social media amplification of the rumor was responsible.[16]

What is revealed and what is hidden by such data-handling are significant. As with prior viruses, it tends to be certain groups in the population who are more vulnerable than others to the infection. As has been shown in many countries, those involved in "frontline" healthcare and essential work – for instance in stores, warehouses or among gig-workers – are hard hit.

Frequently, women are first affected, as their work is often invisible and informal; then other low-income workers; the elderly, especially those in long-term care; low-income wage earners; prisoners; refugees; and migrants. The list is long, but the common feature is that these people are more exposed than others who can more safely isolate at home. It is much more difficult for them to avoid infection because of their work or their responsibilities, or due to enforced proximity – for example, in densely occupied long-term care facilities. Clearly, pandemic surveillance is deeply gendered in intersectional ways – that is, across several dimensions of daily life.

With respect to prisoners, it is even possible that risk is sometimes increased due to using algorithmically biased systems other than ones intended to address the pandemic. In the US, an example comes from "PATTERN," an algorithmic risk assessment tool intended to determine which inmates might re-offend, now being used to say who might be permitted to leave jail for home confinement. The racial bias of this tool has been demonstrated, thus making it even more likely that black people will be made to stay in prison and then develop higher rates of infection and death than others, due to exposure within correctional facilities.[17]

In poorer countries, the situation is often far worse than in richer ones. In this case, the issue might be sheer "data gaps" in pandemic surveillance, rather than skewed data. As Stefania Milan and Emiliano Treré show,[18] many communities in the global south are "in the shadows," unnoticed or only weakly represented in the statistics. Vulnerable populations can easily become even less visible, and their vulnerability exacerbated, by mediocre monitoring, rendering them less eligible for assistance. And to make policy, governments with weak monitoring capacities may use modeling and predictions from elsewhere, which may have the effect of further reducing both awareness of the real situation and the chances of the most needy receiving attention.

It is easy for the lack of reliable information to be accompanied by government misinformation by governments on both the right and the left. Mexico's President Obrador, for instance, assured citizens that during the pandemic they should "keep living life as usual," while Brazil's President Bolsonaro put pandemic concern down to collective "hysteria."[19] Heartbreakingly, these two countries are by far the worst affected in Latin America. By mid-May 2021, Brazil had exceeded half a million deaths, and Mexico 220,000.[20] The invisibility of certain marginalized groups, on the other hand, is something that not only affects specific individuals but also the communities of which they are a part, whether in the global south or the global north.

India has been particularly hard hit by the Coronavirus and, once again, problems of pandemic surveillance are marked here. The response to COVID-19 has in large part been built on the Aadhaar system, a rapidly rolled-out (starting in 2009) national digital identity platform that enrols citizens using biometric data in a centralized system, by far the largest such system in the world.[21] It connects with a massive Public Distribution System (PDS) that was intended to ensure greater access of the poorest to basic necessities. On one hand, population movements were demanded by the government, such as for workers in large cities to return to their villages of origin, which led to greater levels of exclusion from the means of survival. And, on the other, some "point-of-sale" devices – that is, where the benefits are available – were suspended for fear of infection, which has led to persistent insecurity among daily wage-earners.[22]

The issues in India and with Aadhaar are not limited to contact tracing and the increased food insecurity during COVID-19. In early 2021, several millions more enrolled in Aadhaar in preparation for the COVID-19 vaccines.[23] However, in April 2021, Aadhaar was involved in a National Health Authority plan to introduce "contactless COVID-19 vaccine delivery" using Facial Recognition Technology (FRT). The biggest fear of those opposed to this move is that of "exclusion and discriminatory outcomes."[24] It is bad enough, say representatives of ten organizations arguing against this move, that Aadhaar's biometric system has caused exclusion and even starvation deaths, but the unreliable

– and in this context untested – FRT system will likely produce more needless exclusion.

Beyond this are other kinds of differentiation in healthcare on social class lines, that have been apparent in many countries, rich and poor. Take the "wallet biopsies" in the US: paramedics often check patients' wallets before arrival at emergency departments to discover whether they are insured for the procedure required, or to know if they will be accepted at the nearest hospital.[25] Millions of Americans – 17 percent in 2019 – are not insured, relying on Medicaid. As Mirca Madianou notes,[26] comparing the effects of the current pandemic with others, such as Ebola – along with other "natural" disasters such as Hurricane Katrina that killed 1,800 in and around New Orleans in 2005, or Typhoon Haiyan in the Philippines – such events always affect the poor the most. This is now accentuated by the use of digital technologies.

As Madianou also observes, another influence in today's context is surveillance capitalism, and this leads to further forms of pandemic disadvantage. As we saw in chapter 3, the pandemic has prompted an unprecedented shift to digital technologies not only for healthcare "solutions," but also for work, schooling, shopping and socializing. This means that the pressure for profit is strong, right alongside the emphasis on government control of the pandemic. Surveillance capitalism plays an increasing role. The extraction, for profit, of data from everyday transactions and communications, using smartphones, tablets and laptops, lies behind the operation of many platforms, including the wealthiest corporations on the planet.[27]

As surveillance capitalism grows in strength, it works with governments to provide support during the pandemic – think of the Apple–Google liaison for the API that enables the Bluetooth contact tracing apps, for instance – strengthening the government–business ties through such private–public partnerships. This also helps to foster the sense that governments are "doing something," while at the same time distracting attention from the inadequate pandemic preparation by many governments and the insidious undermining of appropriately *public* healthcare that facilitated the unequal effects of the pandemic in the first place.

One may ask, too, where the technical "solutions" came from so quickly? The answer is that an "epidemiological turn in digital surveillance"[28] has been evident for some years and given its moment by the pandemic. Some systems were already in use in development and humanitarian aid, as Linnet Taylor and others say, and were re-packaged for COVID-19.[29] But others came from major corporations. The connections between government initiatives and surveillance capitalism are strengthened by pandemic conditions and may be hard to dismantle when the current crisis has subsided.

Surveillance and inequality in pandemic times

A supposedly reassuring phrase we often hear in our pandemic-stricken world is: "we're all in this together." Of course, it can be an authentic solidarity statement that I wouldn't disparage. However, although we may all be affected, one way or another, really, we're *not* all in this together. The truth is that *how* we are "in this" depends on many factors; the pandemic is far from being a great equalizer. The negative news is that several factors including surveillance *neglect* differences in the population and thus under-estimate the risks to marginalized groups, as we have seen – such as the elderly, racialized and those with low socio-economic status. The even sadder news is that this repeats a historically common pattern.[30]

Some scholars who recognize this fact also argue that the problem – data again – is that current surveillance and reporting of COVID-19 is based on aggregate figures that hide underlying inequalities.[31] They indicate that, as well as factors mentioned earlier in this chapter, some ethnic minority and disadvantaged groups are likely to have "chronic multi-morbidities" – that is, they live with several prolonged illnesses. Such people are less likely to be treated well by medical care systems. Also, pandemic misconceptions and misinformation have circulated more freely among certain minority groups, which reduces the chances of more accurate understanding of current situations. These scholars also propose a data solution: report disaggregated figures, or, in other words, break down the reporting into categories, at least treating the elderly, socially marginalized and racialized differently to highlight their disadvantaged position.

However, such proposed solutions could have problems of their own. Employing them can inadvertently legitimate biological understandings of race. It can also yield opportunities to come to racist responses to the pandemic, rather than attempting to understand the negative working conditions of minorities in various kinds of essential services. Unfortunately, as Sachil Singh[32] shows, once race data is associated with medical conditions and treatment, there is evidence that many doctors see patient illnesses as race-induced rather than looking more for symptoms and specific family histories. If such data is to be collected, he warns, great care should be taken that analysts are aware of the risks. There are no easy answers.

In other circumstances, pandemic surveillance may occur along straightforwardly race-based lines. Take the case of Israel and Palestine, where the Israeli internal security agency, Shin Bet, in a government fiat involving no democratic vote, was empowered to run the contact tracing system that was developed early in the pandemic. Israel has been lauded in many countries for its decisive approach to the pandemic, with lockdowns and then a very efficient vaccination program, which enabled it to open up the economy rapidly, following a significant reduction in cases.

However, this record applies only to Israel – including its constantly expanding illegal settlements – not to Palestine. Both in Gaza, locked-in before the pandemic by the Israeli blockade, and in the West Bank, Palestinians have suffered much more difficult circumstances, especially in the close quarters of refugee camps, such as Aida in Bethlehem and the congested streets of Gaza. And all this was tragically compounded by the ugly armed conflict that broke out in May 2021.

The unequal treatment is nothing new, despite international law requiring occupying powers to ensure the health of those in occupied territory. The effects of the long-standing struggles of Palestinians are clear from the mobilization of secret service security agency Shin Bet to run the contact tracing scheme. This was challenged in court and eventually discontinued.[33] Shin Bet's very existence is predicated on the Palestinian "threat" to Israel, and thus many Jewish Israelis could countenance its cooptation for contagion service, suggests Shaul Duke, because they assumed they would be "non-targets."[34] This is an organization that still uses torture against Palestinian detainees, and imprisons and interrogates children, but it seems that many Israelis are either unaware of or complacent about this.

However, the colonial connection spreads much farther across the globe than only the settler colonialism of Israel. In their reflections on Albert Camus's *La Peste*, Ahmed Kabel and Robert Philippson[35] observe that the humanitarian Camus hardly recognized the colonial dimensions of the Algeria he described. Yet colonialism had much to do with the ways the plague was handled there. Their concern is that the "systemic coordinates of catastrophe" can easily be ignored today, as then, by falling back on the "all in it together" trope. They argue that notions of "capitalist disposability" relate not only to class relations, but also to lives made precarious online, by gender, race and ethnicity. Indigenous people in colonized circumstances are "acutely vulnerable to the ravages of the virus."

While Kabel and Phillipson focus on North Africa, it is important to remember that colonial conditions exist in many countries around the world – in Asia and Latin America but also including in the so-called global north, such as Australia, Canada, New Zealand and the US. Indigenous people are all too familiar with the potentially negative use of surveillance data, including that relating to public health. As one group of scholars points out, "Systemic policies related to genocide and racism, and historic and ongoing marginalization, have led to limitations in quality, quantity, access and use of Indigenous Peoples' COVID-19 data."[36] That data can be both beneficial and harmful, and the frequent exclusion of indigenous people from playing roles in the use of their data is a major obstacle to fair and appropriate surveillance.

Thus, the notion of "disposability" appears at the far end of the spectrum of disadvantages that have been the main focus of this chapter. Clearly, it is vital to consider not only how current conditions enable potentially excessive and unaccountable surveillance, but also who is affected most profoundly by this? Who decides who will live and who will die? Achille Mbembe coined the term "necropolitics" in regard to such disposability. As he argues, race is often central to the power of surveillance, especially in the power of death over "foreign peoples."[37] This reminds us that a critical area for studies of surveillance is to consider the inequitable impact not only of COVID-19 itself, but also of the proffered surveillance involved.

Before concluding this chapter, however, and moving forward to consider what some call the new "pandemic surveillance state," let us take a brief look at the newest dimension of pandemic surveillance, the flashpoint of "COVID passports." Also called "immunity passports," or just mysterious "green passes," these are credentials carried by those who have completed their vaccination course in order to certify that they may enter public places, public transit or airplanes for international travel. They require health and personal identification data, plus a "digital wallet" that can present the credential in the form of a QR code or something similar.[38]

To worries about the privacy and security of such innovations must be added challenges of inequity, discrimination, exclusion and stigmatization. Of course, the travel industry is keen to get people moving again, and economies dependent on tourism want to be first to open their doors to travelers. But the digital identity companies are also eager to ensure that they have a place at the table. Those concerned with providing biometric identifiers have been very active, especially since 9/11,[39] only now they may offer Facial Recognition Technology in addition to other biometrics, or blockchain as an experimental means of running the required software.

However, other questions are also significant. The idea of an "immunity" passport suggests that those who carry one are "safe," but this simplistic binary hides many subtleties. For one thing, no one knows at present how long the effects of the vaccines will last. We are talking about "tendencies" toward safety; these are very soft – in no sense hard – distinctions. And what activities will be permitted, using such a passport? Travel? Attendance at public events? And how might employment opportunities be affected? Whatever questions experts are asked, the key one has to do with inequalities that may be exacerbated by the use of vaccine passports.[40]

The big risk seems to be one of creating social divides

once again, a "two-tier society," as the British Equality and Human Rights Commission[41] put it. Many reasons lie behind "vaccine hesitancy," including a history of mistrust, and concerns about possible side effects that might mean missed work or unexpected healthcare costs. Vaccine passports could be a distraction from broadening vaccination through the population, allowing those vaccinated – generally better off and whiter in Western societies – to insulate themselves from the unvaccinated, and thus decreasing further the chances of vaccination occurring evenly throughout the population.

Or maybe a two-tier world? With the European Union and a number of specific countries planning vaccine passports, the issue is a significant one of global equity. Those with access to vaccines will be favored, and that, by and large, applies to richer countries. And in really low-income countries – say in sub-Saharan Africa – it could take years before people have access to an adequate vaccine supply. True, the WHO has a scheme – COVAX – intended to bridge the rich–poor gap, and already they have started to supply both Ghana and Côte d'Ivoire.[42] But its true worth has yet to be demonstrated.

Stephen Thrasher, writing in the *Scientific American*, seems closer to the mark. He argues for global vaccine equity as being far more important than any vaccines. He has already seen the signs. While, by the start of May 2021, half a billion vaccines had been delivered, that still left more than 7 billion people waiting. Yet in February 2021, governments of some wealthy countries opposed a plan at the World Trade Organization to "waive intellectual property rights on COVID vaccine and medicines so that countries in the global south could manufacture them as quickly as possible."[43] You could be forgiven for thinking that the promised "return to normal" is attractive only to a specific class.

This chapter has explored how pandemic surveillance amplifies social disadvantage, and how it does so along all-too-familiar lines of class, race and gender, within larger capitalist and colonial contexts. It does so via the most basic non-technological means such as informers and "community managers" through to advanced and sophisticated systems of digital technology. The inequalities and inequities of pandemic surveillance are complex and manifold, depending at the largest level on historic injustices, and more recently and locally on inadequacies of digital data collection, analysis and use. These in turn are articulated with recent developments such as the rise of surveillance capitalism, seen especially in the public–private partnerships that have been flourishing during the pandemic.

Each kind of inadequacy calls for far greater care in gathering, handling, analyzing and using data, with a view to seeking and establishing "data justice," which Linnet Taylor sees as "fairness in the way people are made visible, represented and treated as a result of their production of digital data."[44] Needless to say, this is a very different account from those based only on notions of "privacy" and "data protection." It brings to the fore issues of how citizens relate to the state – indeed, of how we live with each other. It recognizes that the shift to the digital – and to surveillance capitalism – is not merely something "technical" (as if the technical ever existed on its own – it manifestly does not), but something that requires new ethical and critical thinking and action, and the mobilizing of appropriate resistance.

As I observed earlier, human flourishing is not defined by any one feature, such as "health," but by several complementary features that also include freedom from excessive government control and full access to the basic resources required for life – food, shelter and human company. All too often, surveillance is viewed merely in relation to its technical or legal aspects. Given its prominence today, in helping to determine life-chances and choices, it should be assessed and judged in terms of human flourishing, within which data justice seems like a good place to begin.

But questions of how to seek data justice and human flourishing are properly debated in the public square, which is itself in crisis mode in many countries. As we have seen, governments around the world have also contributed to the present situation, both positively and negatively. Many fear, for instance, that the surveillance measures prompted by the pandemic will remain in place after the WHO declares that the pandemic is over. Others are concerned that the new alliances between government and corporations will be extended into the post-pandemic world. So before reaching some conclusions about how to imagine a very different post-pandemic world, we have to focus on the new role of what many view as the pandemic-inspired surveillance state.

115

6

Democracy and Power

In 2020 and 2021, corporations and governments the world over engaged in emergency measures to combat COVID-19. Guatemala brought in the military, Israel the security agency Shin Bet, while others deployed police forces to ensure that public health rules were being observed.[1] Facial recognition technologies and drones added ominous surveillance dimensions, while laws and regulations were hurriedly changed or enacted in order to make possible new uses of data for less obvious surveillance, or to contain people in their homes or communities.

In some cases, these tactics had been used before, but in most, bewildered and disoriented populations found themselves in unaccustomed situations in which power was wielded in unfamiliar or intensified ways. In some countries, such as Taiwan or South Africa,[2] resolute action was taken which, despite mistakes, helped to contain contagion. In many countries, however, citizens were subject to the "shock doctrine,"[3] in which national emergencies not only provoke urgent action but are also used as opportunities to acquire or bolster power and deflect democracy.

A common worry, worldwide, was that things could go too far, too fast, and that the temptation to reinforce a "surveillance state" might be too strong for some to resist. *The Economist* warned that "Everything is under control: The state in covid-19."[4] However, in today's pandemic conditions, it is vital to recall that the shock doctrine is about both governments and corporations. The state enables the market, and in a digital world the latter is often the piper playing the tune. The power of platform companies has expanded so much that their role has to be considered alongside that of national governments.

Companies including Apple, Facebook, Amazon and Google have all participated prominently in the pandemic in Western societies – recall the Apple–Google API for digital tracking used in contact tracing. Such liaisons had often been lobbied for previously, and governments in some countries welcomed the potential economic stimulus that companies also bring to their countries.

The corporate–government liaisons can be quite questionable, too. Take, for instance, the role played by Google in "MassNotify," an initiative to alert people to possible COVID exposure in Massachusetts. Google, it seems, while working with Massachusetts Department of Public Health, quietly installed this tracking app onto all Android devices, without user consent. It suffers from several technical and public relations deficiencies, but the sheer lack of transparency is perhaps its major flaw.[5]

At the same time, others such as Alibaba, Tencent and Baidu developed their own responses in China. All these operate in partnership with national governments. On the medical side, for instance, Alibaba offered AI computing capabilities to research institutions to support virus gene sequencing, while Huawei's "WeLink" and Tencent's "WeChat Work" were used for remote working.[6] In the Chinese case, as in the West, such initiatives spill over into international efforts as well. They build on the already existing "Belt and Road" project of establishing infrastructural projects along shipping lanes and across specific land routes across South East Asia, Eastern Europe and Africa, including not only countries such as Sri Lanka and Malaysia but also some of the poorest countries in the world – Pakistan, Laos, Mongolia and Djibouti.[7] Many fear the growth of authoritarianism and loss of civil liberties in *both* East *and* West, as emergency conditions are the pretext for illiberal and less-than-democratic governance.

This chapter is about democracy and power. I deliberately avoid direct reference to the "surveillance state" in the title, just because the COVID-19 pandemic is the first to break out in a surveillance capitalist context.[8] State power is crucial, of course, but now much less frequently on its own. State *and* corporate power work together as never before to create the conditions of pandemic surveillance. Each aspect brings its own challenges to democratic practices, and together their clout is formidable.

The chapter also comes with a caveat. While in a rapid-response book like this, generalizations are made before all the evidence is in, I don't want to give the impression that all governments and corporations are equally undemocratic or pursue power with similar vigor. There is a vast variety, with governments around the world appearing somewhere on a broad spectrum from autocratic diktat to sensitive and well-informed responses to human need, reflected among other ways in their chosen surveillance apparatuses and techniques. As we shall see, some citizens have enjoyed much more participatory relationships with their governments than others.

We begin by commenting on the matter of urgency versus haste in setting up pandemic surveillance schemes, despite the mainly wise advice emanating from the WHO. Secondly, we cannot afford to omit the role of surveillance capitalism and pandemic power, whose relationship we explore a little further. Thirdly, inept and irresponsible government led to some unnecessary or excessive surveillance, producing human rights violations and shriveled civil liberties. Fourthly, we ask questions about emerging issues, such as vaccine passports, that are just becoming lightning rods at the time of writing. Lastly, we address the critical issue of whether the sun will set on pandemic surveillance or whether, as followed 9/11, there will be a substantial legacy of questionable surveillance for another generation to deal with.

Hastily established initiatives

The outbreak of a pandemic demands decisive action. The virus spreads rapidly and, if unchecked, will cause untold suffering and death, plus the long-term disruption of "normal" life for millions, perhaps even altering permanently time-honored patterns of life. Once the virus was identified, international bodies – notably, the WHO – followed their mandate to offer advice on the character of the virus and instruction on what sorts of actions should be taken. What such bodies cannot do, of course, is to require every country to take that advice and instruction. Different polities respond in different ways, reflecting their distinct histories, cultures and political persuasions. The price is high, however, for failure adequately to prepare and act.

In India, for instance, where the first case of COVID-19 appeared on January 30 2020, the response to the WHO's declaration of a pandemic on March 9 was met with a health service reassurance that COVID-19 is "not a health emergency." Then, suddenly, on March 24, Prime Minister Narendra Modi announced that all India would be locked down, within 4 hours of his message to the nation of 1.36 billion. A mass exodus of impoverished people, excluded by employers and landlords, started walking, sometimes hundreds of kilometers, toward their villages and towns of origin.

They were mistreated by police as they walked and then, for fear that the streaming crowds would spread the virus, were turned back at hurriedly contrived state boundary posts, finding their way to miserable encampments in the cities they had just left. The result? Instead of the recommended physical distancing, Arundhati Roy noted, there was "physical compression on an unthinkable scale."[9] Although she has little good to say about the central government response – which was later to include a confusing and controversial message about mandatory contact tracing apps – she acknowledges that some state governments, along with trades unions and groups distributing emergency supplies, showed more acute awareness of the true peril of the crisis. This was also true of Brazil and, indeed, of the United States.

More than a year later, India was once more in the news, with terrifyingly rising infection and death rates, such that in some places cremation facilities were overwhelmed in trying to cope with the number of bodies. In just one Delhi crematorium, Dwarka Sector-24, 413 bodies were cremated between April 19 and April 29, 2021. A proposed pet crematorium, along with local parking lots, had to be redesignated for human bodies as the death toll rose sharply.[10] At the time of writing, India's experience was the third-worst in the world for COVID-19 deaths – over 392,000, many caused by a new variant.[11]

Contrast the Indian response with that of relatively high-income Taiwan. The first COVID-19 case, on January 21, 2020, was a woman in her 50s returning from her teaching job in Wuhan. Taiwan is a densely populated island state of more than 23 million, just 130 km from China. Taiwan responded quickly to the contagion and was well prepared, with a strong public health system and having learned from the experience of SARS in 2003. It boasts a Center for Disease Control that went into action alongside their Central Epidemic Command Center to manage the pandemic.[12]

They immediately screened all passengers arriving from Wuhan, then China, and eventually from all points of origin. In terms of other surveillance, their Infectious Disease Control Act allowed them to connect travel histories with the National Health Insurance Card so that hospitals could identify cases in real time. Plus, personal and government-dispatched phones were used for monitoring quarantine.[13]

In the UK, a Test-and-Trace scheme was established, also early on. It included apps and requirements for infected persons to fill an online form with personal details relating to their contacts.[14] The first app was later replaced by another, based on the Google–Apple API, in September 2020. Rather like the Chinese Health Code, users may scan a QR code at participating venues. In March 2021, the multi-billion-pound schemes, starting with the original Test-and-Trace, were described as not showing evidence that any difference had been made to slowing the pandemic and to preventing further lockdowns.[15] A research article countered this by suggesting that the newer app was itself a success. Interestingly, it also points out that the way people use the app – not approaching close to others, just because they carry the app – may contribute to its success.[16] Self-surveillance may be part of the story – an apt reminder that human involvement in surveillance makes a difference.

The problem with many such systems was that they were rolled out with inadequate preparation. As some observers have argued, such digital technologies for surveillance were "deployed *ad hoc*, without proper impact assessment, stakeholder consultation or evaluation."[17] The fear, then as now, is that governments were too enthusiastic to be seen to be *doing something* and were taking the opportunity to normalize governmental surveillance. Past history, especially following 9/11, shows that such fears are justified. At that time, human rights were often trampled and surveillance was uneven, affecting vulnerable populations disproportionately. Such observations were made by many at the time and in subsequent years, in many countries.[18]

Similarly, warnings about the surveillance risks of excessive haste to utilize surveillance tools were offered early on, for instance by Rob Kitchin, who asked, "Are we rushing into invasive surveillance with immediate and downstream consequences concerning civil liberties, citizenship and surveillance capitalism with little benefit in return?"[19] Indeed, Kitchin's incisive argument, from the evidence he assembled, was that rushed implementations occurred even when shortcomings were apparent. Using the technology, even if it was flawed or unsuitable, was deemed to be better than not using it at all.

Whether or not the hasty deployment of surveillance technologies at the start of the pandemic – or even later on – can be attributed to the shock doctrine analysis remains to be seen. The question calls for serious investigation. But the fact that the rollout of many digital technologies for surveillance purposes was carried out with insufficient care, and even with the deliberate overriding of existing limits on the use of certain systems or laws prohibiting data use for particular purposes, suggests that the shock doctrine hypothesis is worth following up.[20]

Meanwhile, it is worth stressing again that the situation varies enormously around the world, with specific local variations in cultural backgrounds also contributing to the mix. In Japan, for example, the problem for some was not haste but the opposite. The Shinzo Abe government discouraged testing and diagnosis for the virus on an individual level because this would overwhelm local governments, weakened – though this was not mentioned – by decades of under-funding public health.

It seems that, among other things, concerns about losing face over the possibility of postponing the Olympics – planned for 2020 – might have contributed to confusion over how many people were actually infected by the virus. A prominent doctor, Shinji Shimada, accused the government of deliberately making testing difficult, supressing infection data and even deflecting attention from the true cause of death. The government countered this, claiming that cluster-tracing, not individual diagnosis, was their plan.[21]

The situation in South Korea, too, reflects a specific cultural background, at the same time as echoing similar emphases on decisive action (similar in this respect to Taiwan) and reliance on surveillance capitalism. This country, as we saw earlier, instituted testing, contact tracing and clear instructions to citizens from the start. They gathered and analyzed data in determined, systematic fashion. But, while they successfully contained some of the worst effects of the virus, which were all too evident in other countries, their activities, suggests George Baca, were reflective of a more cynical approach.

Baca proposes that the South Korean government "coordinated its pandemic response in ways that have expanded its already formidable technologies for tracing, tracking and mining activities of ordinary citizens."[22] They also enlisted businesses such as CCTV, credit card transactions and telephone companies to complete their surveillance tracing and tracking. This later spread to the use of phone towers, mobile apps and "smart city" sensors. The infamous Shincheonji Church debacle that led to a "super-spreader" event prompted massive stigmatizing of the church, which was used as a warning to all about why they should obey public health instructions.

Baca concludes that "COVID-19 has become a showcase for government agencies and private capital to present their capabilities and control over society as a positive force." In so doing, he says, they deepen South Korea's social contradictions and contribute to an individualism that undermines chances for any collective approach to social change. Yet in an international comparative perspective, it could also be argued that Korea's "individualism" was far more attuned to *social* benefit than that of the US. In an empirical study, Junghwan Kim and Mei-Po Kwan find a strong contrast between personal privacy-oriented Americans, and public benefit-oriented South Koreans, especially in the sensitive area of location-tracking.[23]

Surveillance capitalism, pandemic power

At first sight, the smartphone might appear to be a counter-intuitive instrument for calming COVID-19, but it has indeed proved to be a prominent player.[24] Smartphone use is prominent in three central forms of pandemic surveillance: contact tracing, epidemic modeling and public health communication to counteract the "infodemic" of misinformation unleashed by the global crisis. By December 2020, at least 74 countries had adopted some kind of smartphone app to aid in contact tracing. Some see this as a novel way of managing individual behavior, not only by the state but also by companies, now used to offering incentives, guidance and constraints through everyday smartphone use.[25]

Much of what has been happening within the pandemic relates, then, to the emergence and development of surveillance capitalism, enormously boosted by pandemic conditions. Recall that surveillance capitalism is the process in which what were once thought of as "data fumes," or the exhaust from everyday online activity, became astronomically valuable once their capacity to reveal consumer characteristics could be harnessed. This is done by collecting large quantities of data about people's preferences and choices along with their age, gender, background, education, income, location, movements and so on, in order to sell such information to companies who can use it for advertising, nudging and guiding consumers of their products and services. The mode of prediction, again.

Surveillance scholars have been examining the use of

126

mass surveillance by commercial entities for many years, but Shoshana Zuboff's book *The Age of Surveillance Capitalism*[26] has helped to revive that debate, as we have seen. She focuses especially on the ways in which corporations – especially Google – found ways of making people's inner lives of choice, motivation and commitment legible to their data analysts. In her analysis, the key threat is to individual autonomy. At the same time, while certain freedoms are indeed imperiled, as we saw in chapter 5, surveillance capitalism also contributes to the enlargement of discrimination and gross inequality.

The knowledge gleaned by these corporations is *about* us all, but, Zuboff stresses, it is not *for* us. During a pandemic, however, the same companies can give the impression that the data they accumulate and analyze *can* be "for us." Hence the rush to provide apps to assist in everything from contact tracing, through quarantine monitoring, to depression alleviation. That this echoes what happened two decades ago, after 9/11, is hardly surprising, only now the range of tools is offered not only to governments but to many other organizations and, indeed, right down to the individual level.

Some basic injustices arise from surveillance capitalism, notes Jonathan Cinnamon. It's not just that people are separated from their data, which then is fuel for corporate profit – an injustice of *maldistribution* – but also that people are *misrecognized* due to the algorithmic processing and categorizing of their data, and then *misrepresented* by the same data. The latter renders them voiceless and thus unable to challenge these misuses of their data.[27] Crucially, Cinnamon concludes that these "abnormal" practices undermine the very chances of equality in everyday life within any given polity.

There are real risks here, not just for individual autonomy, but also for social and political arrangements, especially for democracy. The "shock doctrine" idea warns that governments of almost every stripe may use emergency situations as opportunities to consolidate their power and this can be either blatant or, more likely, subtle, and mixed with other motivations. But now this is buttressed by corporate practices that further weaken democratic opportunities.

The democratic deficit may be seen not only in "command economy" moves or in draconian control of population movement – which might be justified by governments as the means of stalling the explosive spread of the virus – but also in the failure to draw on the resourcefulness of the population to organize pandemic resources or to participate in decisions about the use of apps or monitoring devices such as drones or fixed cameras.

This may be illustrated by the Brazilian case. Unlike South Korea, which rapidly accepted the reality of the COVID-19 threat, and more in line with the Trumpian disdain for public health advice, Brazilian authorities, under Jair Bolsonaro, were fatefully dismissive of medical and epidemiological caution. The president claimed that slowing the economy in any way would cause more deaths than any pandemic.[28] Health ministers who recognized the gravity of COVID-19 or disagreed with the president's quick-fix solutions were dismissed from their posts.

The results in Brazil show an extremely mixed story of very high infection and death rates. Some urban zones and national regions are affected much less than others. Higher sickness and death rates overwhelmingly affect the poorer areas such as the urban *favelas*, but also reflect uncoordinated efforts at contact tracing in wealthy areas, often initiated by corporations. One start-up, inLoco, switched from location marketing services to monitoring the self-isolation of residents in cities that contracted them to do so. Another initiative using smartphones was launched in the northern state of Bahia, in an area with the strongest opponents of Bolsonaro. Monitora Covid sent information about health status and personal information to a central platform in that area.

Researchers Rafael Evangelista and Rodrigo Firmino also show how the pandemic prompted other kinds of surveillance in Brazil – for example, accelerating the use of educational platforms relating to learning at home. Google, prominently, signed contracts with 70 percent of state universities in 2020, compared with 11 percent in 2019. At present, it seems clear that it is the priorities and practices of social media and "platform capitalism" – with its commercial aims of selling user data and capturing markets – that dominate these initiatives. The educational task, as understood by its academic proponents, takes second place.[29]

Having said that, it is equally true that pandemic conditions elsewhere have also contributed to the rapid growth of surveillance capitalism in educational contexts. This was touched on in chapter 3, "Domestic Targets," but it is worth adding here that most of the platforms in use in North America and elsewhere are also guided primarily by profit. Ron Deibert rightly observes that "Largely without public debate – and absent any new safeguards – we've become more dependent on a technological ecosystem that is notoriously insecure, poorly regulated, highly invasive and subject to serial abuse."[30]

It is also worth noting, lastly, that surveillance capitalism is now marked not only by its reliance on Big Data, but also by its championing of the means of analyzing and mobilizing that data – Machine Learning and Artificial Intelligence. Alibaba – the corporation, not a public health agency – for instance, developed an AI system for rapid coronavirus detection from CT scans with 96 percent accuracy. As Carmel Shachar and others point out, however, challenges presented by ML and AI – "from privacy to discrimination to access to care" – come from organizations comprised of *both* government and corporate actors.[31] While rights such as freedom of movement or access to due process have traditionally been conferred by governments on citizens, under what terms might these be upheld by corporate AI bodies? Calls for new codes of ethics point in the right direction, but they have limitations in practice.

Civil liberties, human rights and privacy at risk

As we have seen, surveillance developments – aided by surveillance capitalism – can easily be mobilized to strengthen the power of a given state to control its citizens. We live in a world that has seen a rapid rise in populist authoritarianism in recent years, and surveillance is a tool that may be wielded to assert such new powers. China's responses to the pandemic show how a massive reliance on surveillance – including, and especially, through *corporate* entities such as the well-known Alipay system – can produce not only quickly lowered infection rates, which is highly desirable, but also even deeper daily control of its citizens.

One blogger on Zhihu commented, on the Health Code system initiated in China for the pandemic, that he had anticipated that "the days when humans are ruled by machines and algorithms won't happen for at least the next fifty years." But "the coronavirus epidemic has suddenly brought it on early."[32] Many note that human rights are at risk in China, with little by way of the protections enjoyed by some in other parts of the world. They lack privacy legislation, or even an independent legal system. More widely, there is no free press or strong civil society.

How the Health Code works is opaque to its users. Categories including "having been in an affected area recently" or, even more vaguely, "belonging to groups relevant for the pandemic" can turn the code red. This is fertile soil for the growth of misrecognition and misrepresentation mentioned above. This does not mean, however, that life in all regions of China should be judged in the same light. And nor does it mean that there are no voices for change and greater participation.[33] The present geopolitical context encourages us to suggest that terms like "authoritarian" should be used with care.

As other relevant research shows, how China's

activities are judged varies. It is all too easy to describe
a state as authoritarian and extend that to saying its
surveillance is also authoritarian. Iran is often described
as an authoritarian state. But, as Azadeh Akbari points
out, Iran's COVID-19 experience contrasts with that of
China. While, under other circumstances, Iran might
have followed China's example, due to several extenu-
ating factors it did not. Due to its patchy digital
infrastructure, among other things, Iran was unable to
use surveillance technologies on a large scale, as other
countries have, against COVID-19.[34]

Back in China, we have observed several times that
the COVID-19 surveillance technologies have served
to strengthen state control of both individuals and
whole population groups. But, as Casiano, Haggerty
and Bernot note, these very developments seem to
have sparked the emergence of a new kind of "circum-
scribed individual autonomy" among Chinese citizens.[35]
For, they point out, the massive Health Code system
also encourages citizens, through new forms of self-
governance, to "experience 'freedom' in a 'society of
control.'" This might also help to explain why many
Chinese are content with – even proud of – China's
response.

Equally, care should also be taken with the term
"democratic." As we have seen, countries that claim
to be democratic – such as India and Israel – have
also used methods of pandemic surveillance that one
could be forgiven for assuming are more appropriate in
authoritarian contexts. I have in mind the "mandatory"
Aarogya Setu contact tracing app, and its connections with Aadhaar as a tool of state control in India,

or the use of Israel's security agency, Shin Bet, to organize their contact tracing program. In each case, the current government's favoring of a specific group, with ethno-religious roots, is a significant factor skewing "democratic" practice.

The pandemic has also been used as an opportunity for buttressing and extending already existing surveillance-control in some countries, including Japan. A new Digital Agency was proposed in September 2020, intended to extend the centralized ID system "My Number Card," and link it with health, education and other information, as well as with municipalities and some commercial enterprises. Indeed, the initiative came from leaders of industry, too. The Digital Agency would enable the linking and analyzing of knowledge of, say, health and eating habits, or income and education, on an individual basis. The Bill to create the Digital Agency passed in the Japanese Diet on May 12, 2021.[36]

Civil liberties and human rights have also been curtailed in many countries during the pandemic. Some have used quite "authoritarian" surveillance to combat the pandemic, while others used COVID as a cover for restricting specific rights. A report from the Civicus Monitor[37] shows that European countries such as Hungary, Poland, Serbia and Slovenia clamped down on freedoms, while Uganda targeted LGBTQ+ people, and in India informal workers were further violated by the state. The US was also singled out as an offender, as were Chile, Costa Rica and Ecuador.

The creation of new means of documenting where people are, where they have been and their health status, along with data-modeling to track the spread of the virus, exploits in unprecedented ways data that would otherwise be subject to privacy and data protection legislation. This data is peculiarly sensitive for many reasons. It could be the backdrop or catalyst for scapegoating or racism, for example, or could needlessly restrict civil liberties such as freedom of movement, beyond what is required for protecting lives during the pandemic. What one might consider necessary self-discipline – such as wearing a mask, or not mingling with unknown others – could be bolstered by systems that actually direct behavior.[38]

This can extend within different demographic groups and classifications, such as essential workers, making the distribution of these measures very uneven. Once systems designed for one purpose "creep" over to another – justified by the extraordinary circumstances – it is easy for these to become permanent features of the governance context, as happened with post-9/11 "security" regimes.[39]

One feature of government responses to the pandemic has been policies of information control, and this has been evident in both democracies and autocracies. This certainly raises questions about civil liberties and human rights. While some governments have taken steps to try to criminalize those creating and distributing "fake news" during the pandemic, they themselves have sometimes contributed to the distribution of misleading or inaccurate information. Some have also restricted access to government information. Either way, surveillance may be the first move, in that the monitoring of communication is the most efficient way of discovering what information is circulating.[40]

In all these ways and others, then, civil liberties and human rights have been imperiled during the pandemic, in both "authoritarian" and "democratic" societies. This is visible not just in one area, but often over several different aspects of social and political life. In India, again, it is evident not only in the uncertainties but also in the "constant talk of 'war' against the virus and treating the issue as a law-and-order problem rather than a public health crisis." Indians are "witnessing a suspension of civil rights, judicial oversight, and a lack of informed debate."[41]

Emerging issues

Since the 1930s, the WHO, or its predecessor bodies, has issued "yellow cards – *cartes jaunes*" as a means of indicating, for travel purposes, that users have been vaccinated against various diseases. I have had to use one for traveling in India and some South East Asian countries. But these are paper documents, not digital ones. New-style COVID-19 vaccination certificates are already in use in Israel and France, among other countries, and Air New Zealand is trialing the International Air Travel Association (IATA) "Travel Pass" as I write.[42]

But these digital "passports" are much more controversial, both for the actual data they contain and for their potential for discrimination. Items such as the Digital Immunity Certificate or the European Union's "Digital Green Pass" would be useful for accurately determining whether people have been vaccinated or not, but they could easily become a form of immunity privilege for the wealthy to travel. The idea of creating "immunity" passes does not make sense. Having had a vaccine does not make one "immune" from becoming infected; it's just less likely that you become really sick or die from COVID-19. That leaves two other options: a digital document to prove you have tested negative for COVID-19, and evidence of having had a vaccination.

There is plenty of pressure for such things, of course. The tourism industry is eager to open up travel, local communities would like to lift COVID restrictions on eating out or attending public events. As the *New York Times* put it, "Governments typically talk about [passes] as a way to open up economies. Individuals, as a way to re-enter normal life. Public health experts, as a way to reduce transmissions."[43] And, as well as local or regional authorities' involvement, companies like IBM are also in the game – in IBM's case, with a "Digital Health Pass" built on their blockchain technology.[44]

But rollouts are complicated by many things. Agreement about which vaccines are acceptable is one. For instance, South Africa is not using its own AstraZeneca vaccine because it's less effective against the South African strain of COVID-19. Other countries have failed to agree on which vaccines are effective. As digital documents, such passes need extensive privacy and security protections, and restrictions on potential uses. Above all, they will need internationally shared standards, upon which agreement could take years.

In Western countries, white and well-off groups tend to get vaccinated first, which is already producing great inequalities, which will almost inevitably be reflected in pass-use. At the other end of the spectrum, refugees and asylum-seekers are likely to face nearly insurmountable barriers to obtaining such passports, not least because they often have to destroy their ID documents when fleeing their original homeland. As having a vaccine passport is evidence of vaccination, this could also be problematic. In Australia, for instance, current policies may exclude refugees from access to vaccine passports.[45]

These passes, then, could also contribute to further discrimination, prejudice and stigma. Many – such as the 1 billion or more, globally, who have no passport, national ID, driver's licence or even birth certificate – will never have this kind of electronic document. And, like most other issues discussed here, for pass holders, they are by definition surveillant. Carriers of vaccine passports are made visible, represented and treated according to the data that the documents contain.

No sunset for pandemic projects?

Two decades ago, following 9/11, considerable debate arose over the need for "sunset clauses" on the exceptional surveillance and security measures set in place to try to thwart terrorism, especially in travel contexts. Such clauses were to ensure that the emergency measures, the "states of exception," temporarily invoked to deal with an unprecedented situation, would not last beyond a certain fixed date.

By 2019, 12 of the 15 "emergency measures" in the infamous US PATRIOT Act were not only still in force, they had also gained the status of permanent law.

The secret warrantless and illegal surveillance program covering American citizens in contact with anyone in Afghanistan, initiated 3 days after September 11, 2001, and revealed by whistleblower Edward Snowden, was also made "legal" in 2019.[46]

Many fear that the extraordinary legal changes and deeply surveillant measures following the pandemic will meet the same fate. "Why let a crisis go to waste?" seems to be the mantra of the shock doctrine exponents. And while members of the public might have forgotten the aftermath of 9/11, in terms of enlarged and entrenched surveillance, those concerned with civil liberties and human rights are all too aware of the current risks.

In the UK, for example, the government plans to retain the personal data it has acquired during the pandemic, for 20 years, while denying that individuals have any right to deletion of their records. Rights groups fear that the data will be used for other purposes, observing that, in the first place, the government failed to make a data protection impact assessment before data collection and analysis began.[47] The pressure comes from those who benefit from the new situation, primarily from having access to more data, valuable either for profit or for ongoing policy-fulfilment.

The idea that "function creep" – or, in this case, "mission creep" – could occur currently seems highly likely, especially given the fact that both state and commerce stand to benefit. The term "function creep" describes situations in which some surveillance system – say, CCTV established for anti-vandalism purposes – is extended to deal with, say, drug trafficking offenses. "Mission creep," on the other hand, refers to surveillance set up for one large-scale task, being re-purposed for another quite different task. Contact tracing systems, for instance, could be re-used for ongoing public health monitoring in non-pandemic circumstances.

An example is that of the Thai–Myanmar border being monitored by drones and ultra-violet cameras after 16 people crossed the border illegally during 2020. What began as a pandemic exercise appears to be becoming permanent. Apps tracking COVID-19 patients' every move, or cameras installed in Australian homes to check that quarantine conditions are being maintained – these too could enjoy a longer shelf life than originally envisaged. Despite falling infection rates in Russia, CCTV and facial recognition scans are still in use.[48]

An especially disturbing example comes from Israel, where, during the crackdown on Palestinian protesters and the attacks on Gaza in May 2021, Shin Bet – the security agency that organized contact tracing – appeared to have used the same technical systems, normalized for COVID-19, to track and monitor protesters. Those who attended protests against the expropriation of Palestinian homes by Jewish Israeli settlers received phone messages that read: "You have been identified to have taken part in violent acts at Al-Aqsa Mosque. We will hold you accountable – Israeli Intelligence."[49]

A plausible rationale for mission creep might be that the situations conducive to pandemic outbreaks remain. The prospects are that, given the ongoing conditions favoring the eruption of zoonotic disease, for example, other pandemics – perhaps worse ones – could break out, for which we would do well to be ready. But if legal exceptions have to be made, little time would be wasted if plans were made to revive some regulatory relaxation only when necessitated by the new emergency. Such questions would have to be wrestled with very carefully.

In one last case, as well as setting up a symptom-tracing app in Ghana, the government there also passed legislation to enhance the powers over telecommunications systems during public emergencies. This Executive Instrument (EI) was described as a response to an "urgent need" for a "means of tracing all contacts of persons ... actually affected by a public health emergency."[50] But the EI also requires a centralized registry for mobile equipment identities – that is, a national database matching individuals to phone numbers, plus those numbers to phone models. The passing pandemic seems to have parented a permanent surveillance system of some power. Despite a Ghanaian Data Protection Act and Data Protection Commission, it will take concerted civil society and political action to ensure that this new power is not abused.

Much surveillance development has occurred without what many would consider appropriate democratic discussion and involvements. Some shock doctrine tactics may have long-term implications. A country such as Ghana may be able to flex its political muscles to prevent problems associated with long-term legacies of what started out as pandemic procedures. Time will tell. But democracy is definitely challenged right now.

Yet another country, New Zealand, both invoked strong government, under Prime Minister Jacinda Ardern, producing policy responses that were both stringent and comprehensive, and remained transparent and accountable. True, New Zealand's population is only 4.9 million, and relatively wealthy, but nonetheless the prime minister enjoys popular support and respect for her actions. The government has endeavored to keep the public informed about the pandemic and the response.[51]

What remains to be seen is how far efforts to keep excessive and unnecessary surveillance in check will withstand the extra dimension that surveillance capitalism adds to conventional government control with its all-too-common shock doctrine propensities. The prospects are varied, but also volatile, given these relatively new potentials. They call for some serious reflection – not to mention action – on the part of civil society, and indeed of all citizens. How to approach such a post-pandemic world, in human-centered and yet planetary ways, is the topic of the concluding chapter.

7
Doorway to Hope

Who is the *Pale Rider*? It was Laura Spinney's investigation of the 1918 global pandemic that used this title. The pale rider, found in an African-American song – "pale horse, pale rider, done taken my true love away…" – is a common trope for Death, the fourth horse-rider of the Apocalypse in the biblical book of Revelation. Among other dire descriptors, the COVID-19 pandemic has been discussed in apocalyptic terms.[1] But, while apocalypse is often taken to be a synonym for something like "catastrophe," the word "apocalypse" – Greek, *apokaluptein*, literally, "uncover" – adds to that the sense of an unveiling, a laying bare of what was previously unseen or unrecognized.

In the original biblical context of the "Pale Rider," apocalyptic writing is intended to shake people out of complacency, conventional wisdom and commonplace assumptions, to question the way things are done, to puncture pernicious practices, to probe political platitudes. But beyond that, it exists to create space for other ways of seeing the world, to open doors to fresh futures, especially ones beyond the monstrous grip of commercial and coercive powers. Now, I make no pretence of offering a properly apocalyptic reading of pandemic surveillance.[2] But having tried to provide some clues about what has been uncovered by the pandemic, I'll hint at what sorts of futures are worth working toward, and hoping for.

Having lambasted the lamentable opportunism of the shock doctrine, I should explain why – perhaps paradoxically – I too see the pandemic as opportunity. The shock doctrine is a perversely poignant parody of another way forward, involving ordinary people in everyday life, working together for the common good. You have already heard some of their voices earlier, and here I give them rightful prominence. Their quest is not for power so much as for the flourishing of all. It is guided, not by optimism based in technical–commercial prowess, but by hope for a humanly livable world.

Plenty of commentators have pinpointed ways in which the pandemic has exposed tragic aspects of contemporary life – the scandalously sorry state of long-term care facilities, in which so many have died, being one of the earliest noted in Ontario, as in many other places. Such situations, though heartbreaking and horrible, pale in comparison when contrasted with the desperate conditions in the impoverished *favelas* of Brazil or the street workers in India's sprawling cities, where COVID has devastated communities and where bodies were piled awaiting cremation. Sadly, some pandemic surveillance has served to worsen such conditions. Mistakes, bad choices, hasty action – all these and more have been prominent.

Moments of apocalyptic disclosure range from the wide-angle global nature of surveillance processes in the twenty-first century through to the invisible ways in which data is analyzed and utilized by means of algorithms. What is revealed all too often turns out to be a powerful system of collusion between governments and platform companies around the world, through potent means of data-handling that may diminish both human freedom and fairness. Tech-solutionism and haste are striking features of how the pandemic is handled and managed.

This raises questions of how far everything from contact tracing apps to large-scale health data systems are fit for purpose, on the one hand, and promote fairness and freedom, on the other. Of course, these queries spread to non-health-related aspects of pandemic surveillance, too. Companies such as Amazon and Alibaba will likely continue to prosper from pandemic conditions, as John Milbank and Adrian Pabst say, "like vultures circling over wounded prey."[3] Unless some dramatic changes occur, surveillance will be a means of control both through credit and security arrangements, not to mention through the activity of employers, educators and marketers who learned new ways of remotely tracking millions during the pandemic.

Governments have restricted rights and curtailed movement, changed laws and brought in the armed forces or security agencies to attempt to deal with the changing situation of the pandemic. Some actions have been heavy-handed and clumsy, others have met with popular approval for their promptness and apparent success.

When it comes to data-handling, however, much is left to be desired in many countries. Contact tracing apps, for instance, have been a mixed blessing. Considerable credit has been given to them for their role in alerting people to their contact with infection, but their broader usefulness has often been compromised, by everything from false positives or negatives through to inadequate take-up rates that might have produced a wider usefulness for understanding and responding to the pandemic's specific paths.

Overall, the surge of surveillance-gone-viral would justify the *double-entendre* "pandemic surveillance." As well, COVID-19 has itself mutated, producing variants, or new strains, raising renewed public health challenges. While this is characteristic of RNA viruses, some scientists try to reproduce the process – called "gain-of-function, GOF" research – in the lab, in order to understand virus behavior better. But what if an errant virus escapes the lab? When president, Barack Obama shut down GOF research until clear ethical rules were available.[4]

The fear of "function creep" is evident in pandemic surveillance, as noted especially in the previous chapter, and this seems to mimic some aspects of gain-of-function in virology.[5] Those experimental tech "solutions" hastily invented for pandemic purposes could well escape into long-term use, or even be mistaken for "normal" or "necessary" surveillance, despite their demonstrable downsides. To avoid this, properly ethical direction, along with legal limits and internationally agreed regulation, as well as public vigilance by civil society, will be required.

This book as a whole deals with the "uncovering" aspect of apocalypse, revealing significant and sometimes searing aspects of pandemic surveillance that might have been missed by some. The focus in what follows is not so much on what has been "uncovered" as on responses to what we now see. How may pandemic surveillance be seen in a different light – of what could be? And are there cracks where the light might get in? Let me suggest some answers from stories of two countries.

A tale of two countries

Rather than focus on "usual suspect" countries in North America and Europe, I draw attention to two contrasting situations, one in Latin America and the other in Asia, in which ordinary citizens played a role in letting in the light. Each has been mentioned earlier – Taiwan, a close neighbor of China, for its prompt successful action against the virus; and Brazil, for its mimicking Trump-style indifference and mockery of medical advice with its consequent loss of life, especially among the urban poor.

Taiwan (population 23.57 million), by all accounts, has done well in its efforts to counter the worst effects of the pandemic. Its story is in many respects markedly different from that of many other countries, and the role of civil society, radical transparency and a government deemed trustworthy has much to do with it. "Civic tech hacktivists" played a critical role, along with the young Digital Minister, Audrey Wang, representing the government. In Taiwan, "there is a strong collective narrative of digital democracy and government and civil society work together in online spaces to build public trust."[6]

Against a backdrop of concern for the growing power of its near neighbor, China, the Sunflower Movement (2014) was the first sign of serious hacker-power, organizing against a threatening trade deal. This developed into a movement that monitored carefully what was happening in China – hence their early warning, thanks to a senior health scientist, in December 2019 of the new virus detected in Wuhan. Almost immediately, crowd-sourced work began to ensure that what would be needed was known about by the public. "Reverse procurement" was how Wang described the bottom-up scanning for available masks and other anti-virus necessities.

They also foresaw the likelihood of misinformation and thus mobilized the government to work against it, using memes and short positive messaging in a policy of "humor over rumor." In other words, from the outset, data was used in very different ways from that in many other countries, making the civic hackers central players in a very different scenario from others described in this book. This "experimental application of digital infrastructure" as Kelsie Nabben[7] depicts it, has been the basis of the Taiwanese pandemic response. This includes platforms of public policy participation to allow community voices to be heard.

It should be noted that Taiwan's government as a whole has not enjoyed a high level of trust, but the handling of the pandemic has produced, by contrast, a 91 percent satisfaction rate with the Central Epidemic Command Center – which was itself activated on January 20, 2020, the rapid response being critical for Taiwan's success. The CECC was headed by medical experts, rather than government or military officials. They engaged in data-sharing between departments of National Health and National Immigration, and monitored quarantine from the outset.[8] But these measures seem to have been acceptable in the climate of imaginative responses, even though Amnesty International chides the country gently on its possible neglect of privacy practices in data-sharing.

What the story of Taiwan's civic hacktivists and Audrey Tang shows is that "promoting openness and transparency nurtures mutual trust"[9] between citizens and government. The key, for most observers, was the cooperative interaction between government and civil society at several levels. This in turn opened the door to fresh possibilities for other forms of collective action to blossom. The story is very different in Brazil.

Note that, at around 210 million, Brazil has almost ten times the population of Taiwan. At the start of the pandemic, analysts perceived three possible paths.[10] "Rupture" meant that historic inequalities and asymmetries of wealth would rapidly be worsened by the pandemic crisis. "Exception" would treat as temporary the pandemic and its consequences, promoting a rapid return to "normality." "Acceleration" entailed speedy adoption of "surveillance capitalist" technologies for mass isolation and the transposition of work and learning to the internet.

As they concluded, President Bolsonaro's policies of exception and acceleration produced many further harms – including 507,000 deaths at the time of writing – without any of the promised benefits. He actively opposed the Ministry of Health's comprehensive and integrated plans to deal with disease, even proposing spurious medications such as hydroxychloroquine. And while aid was available for those who lost incomes, receiving aid depended on being electronically registered in a new level of enrollment, which is difficult when around one third of the population – mainly those who most need assistance – has inadequate access to the internet, limited to phones.

New biometric registration methods were used as well, including facial recognition. This is despite the fact that more than 50 percent of the population is black (*preto*) or mixed (*pardo*) and that facial recognition technologies are notoriously poor at properly capturing populations of African origin. Those in poverty include a majority of black people. But the ruling elites have a history of indifference to those who make up the poverty-stricken swathes – and who often depend on platforms, in delivery roles – especially in megacities such as São Paulo.

Within this bleak picture, however, evidence of oppositional movements offers some light. Of course, the Brazilian government used platform companies to organize the heatmaps of urban areas, showing where more people than permitted were congregating, as well as to track movement and check the maintaining of physical distance. The government thus drew on expectations of personal behavior to make their governing

149

more effective – as theorist Michel Foucault might explain it – thus policing people's self-care.

Yet citizens also responded critically, despite the heavy policing that developed during the pandemic. Some criticized the lack of privacy protection for the data being transferred wholesale to scarcely regulated companies. At least one lawyer made a public complaint, calling for a collective *habeas corpus*, while many found ways to self-protect by eluding surveillance and avoiding social media tracking. Others, in academic and technical contexts, also raised questions.[11]

One concerns the lack of transparency regarding the details of the new, data-based surveillance methods, especially as the organizations concerned are platform and tech companies. Another misgiving relates to questions of anonymization – the claim that data used in striving to stem the pandemic tsunami would not be identifiable. One resourceful investigative journalist actually succeeded in deanonymizing supposedly safe data, using a triangulation method – and it transpired that those whose names came up had no idea how far their information had traveled.

The third issue that was targeted by critics was the fact that the "new" surveillance measures were actually built on previously existing platforms. One such allowed São Paulo police to map crime spots, which had already been augmented with video surveillance for tracing suspects and raising real-time alerts. All three kinds of questions have ramifications, not only for policing the pandemic in the present, but also for potential long-term uses of the same technologies for population control.

Civil society groups in Brazil, including Data Privacy, Internet Lab and the Internet Steering Committee, have spoken out against the expansion of questionable surveillance. They actively promote principles for limiting new surveillance measures, based on the General Data Protection Law. These same groups have been working for years to promote civil liberties in the face of surveillance threats and were behind the "Marco Civil da Internet" (Internet Civil Rights framework) in 2014. In April 2020, they launched a podcast on "Datocracy," proposing a debate on the appropriate use of personal data in the pandemic. In the same year, Data Privacy Brazil issued a report on "Privacy and the pandemic," proposing a consistent line of resistance against the indiscriminate use of monitoring systems.

In other words, behind the screaming headlines about the appalling loss of life, especially among the most marginalized in Brazil, are groups and movements that try to hold the government to account. Activist organizations have succeeded in alerting Brazilians to the risks associated with pandemic surveillance, based on evidence and expertise. Academics and journalists have added weight to the resistance, too.

Beyond apocalypse

The process of "laying bare" reveals not only negatives – the feared normalization of surveillance[12] – but also some positive aspects that are worth maintaining and nurturing. In the above tales from two countries, I suggest the following are worth pondering further.

Ordinary people without any claims to power made a difference in their own situations. They worked together to confront pandemic realities with alternative ways forward rather than merely falling back on standard offerings of public–private partnerships, which often depend heavily on powerful platforms for leadership.

They often saw the situations as already compromised by deeply divided populations – ones in which the poor, disadvantaged and marginalized were suffering much more than the comfortable, internet-savvy classes that could, for instance, switch more readily to working and schooling at home. Indeed, they didn't necessarily start at a "population" level at all, but with those in varied positions of need. As Linnet Taylor insists, an ethics of care should guide pandemic priorities.

Population data comes from many sources and is far from comprehensive, meaning that its accuracy and reliability are questionable. In many countries, there was also a "utilitarian calculation"[13] about how many people in a given country might die as a result of the disease. The uncertainties and missing data could be better thought of, suggests Taylor, not as "gaps" in information but as *people* likely to be members of less visible groups, with less access to benefits such as healthcare.

These would include low-wage workers, the elderly, migrants, prisoners and visible minorities. Taylor's approach is *embodied*, asking what such people actually need and what their relationships are with each other, rather than the approach of population-based management. Location-tracking using smartphones is a blunt instrument for knowing what people are actually doing and, in any case, as Taylor says, "less-visible groups also tend to be those who conform less to the norms of behaviour on which data analytics are predicated."

In both Taiwan and Brazil – and elsewhere – each kind of inadequacy calls for far greater care in gathering, handling, analyzing and using data, with a view to seeking and establishing "data justice," as discussed in chapter 5. This assumes – but also goes well beyond – practices based only on notions of "privacy" and "data protection."

Other important elements of what is revealed in situations such as those in Taiwan and Brazil include the emphasis on transparency. Governments of whatever stripe – not to mention corporations, which also wish to guard their secrets – often have poor records of transparency. In March 2020, along with 100 other organizations, the EFF called on governments to be transparent about their COVID-19 arrangements. They noted that "it's neither normal nor healthy for democracy to hide or classify public health-related decisions or deliberations."[14]

Yet, as we have seen, many governments act in a clandestine fashion, making key decisions behind closed doors, or changing legal requirements for matters such as how health data is handled by embedding them in other legislation. And this happens in democracies, as well as in more authoritarian settings. Not being transparent leaves ordinary citizens in the dark about what is happening, but it also disables peoples' capacity to discuss publicly issues that touch – literally – on their life-chances.[15]

Public trust in government is crucial to the effective working of digital systems established to counteract the pandemic,[16] as was seen in Taiwan, where the government was perceived as *trustworthy*.[17] The Mexican government lost citizen trust in November 2020, when a mandatory program using QR swiping for contact tracing appeared. The lack of democratic process prompted the former Data Protection Commissioner to suggest that citizens resist.[18]

But care has to be taken – transparency can also be subverted to facilitate neoliberal agendas. David Pozen shows that transparency is never a "thing," but a social process: a means, not an end.[19] Specific contexts have to be taken into account, in sociological fashion. Transparency serves other goals, such as accountability, which is essential for trust – another feature mentioned in the Taiwan story. It can also serve the cause of data justice.

Yet another feature of the above stories – especially in Taiwan – is the role of computer scientists and software engineers, who were the frontline hacktivists. Using their skills imaginatively to further aims of directly aiding the public health agencies and the procurement of essential supplies no doubt contributed to the sense of mutual trust. But, at best, this can also lead to the production of better systems, which are clearly socially responsible.

All too often, as Norma Möllers[20] shows, computing science and software design – now deeply involved with building algorithms, including for AI and ML – are taught and understood as practices removed from the real world. Students dissociate their work from actual "applications," and disengage from any sense that their work involves politics. Those who would question pandemic surveillance need to form strategic alliances with computer scientists who see their vocation not merely as having "add-on" ethics, but as an intrinsically critical task.

Lastly, the movements questioning excessive and ill-planned surveillance in Brazil have a sense of partnership with those working in legal and regulative bodies. This is vital, especially for post-pandemic situations, in which great vigilance will be called for in checking that "emergency" measures are dismantled or properly regulated. The NGOs have direct contact with those affected by needless or coercive surveillance, but they also relate to other bodies pressing for appropriate limits to and guidelines for appropriate surveillance.

Data protection, information and privacy agencies exist in many countries and they have an essential role in acting as watchdogs to monitor the legality of surveillance operations of both government and corporation and to promote the development of fresh and up-to-date laws governing the just and proper handling of data. Are new uses of data really necessary, and are they proportional to the need? These are the kinds of questions that regulators have to pose regarding any data collection and analysis, especially new or "emergency" kinds.

Sharing aggregate data from platform companies is a key issue, here. In Brazil, the government actually handed some central public health tasks to the platforms themselves, outsourcing what has conventionally been seen as properly the role of public health agencies.

However, in other countries, the waters have been muddied by the involvement of private companies in health data handling, sometimes with an accompanying secrecy about what actually goes on within pandemic-inspired coalitions.

As Teresa Scassa and others argue, this is exactly the time to be taking even more care with this precious data, referring as it does to living people whose management at the hands of the relevant agencies will depend on how they are made visible, represented and treated. Again, de-identification is crucial. But many other legal issues are also raised, such as how tracking apps and systems are used, given their inherent privacy-invasive character. As Scassa says, privacy need not be a barrier to seeking solutions for pandemic problems. But "privacy rights, framed by concepts of necessity and proportionality, can – and should – shape data-driven responses."[21]

Pandemic as portal

Arundhati Roy invites us to see the pandemic as a "portal." The door to the post-pandemic future is an open one, not closed to the predatory actions of the public–private partnerships of surveillance capitalism[22] or the tech-solutionism and "dataism" of trust in *la technique*, as Jacques Ellul called it back in the 1950s.[23] Ellul saw technology as something that was being wrenched out of its place as a human strategy for opening up the possibilities of the planet, of overcoming obstacles and limits – and becoming an end in itself, an idol.

Past pandemics have "forced humans to break with the past and imagine the world anew," says Roy. This one is no different. Where surveillance is needed in the new world, it could be guided not by the imperative to extract profit or to exert control, or by belief in the power of Big Data, but by the requirements of human flourishing. And by ordinary people grasping opportunities to work with others for the common good – including a place for surveillance.[24] And that goal can only be sought by refocusing from "technology" to "humanness."

For all data-related activities, in which surveillance is a major player, the frame should be a *human one*, not primarily technological. That is to say, technology should be built for human need – indeed, for human flourishing – and not vice versa. It sounds like a truism, but the in-your-face evidence of this book shows that it needs to be said. So often during the pandemic, excitement over new technological possibilities seems to have overshadowed their task – of mitigating the effects of the pandemic and improving the chances for human benefit.

At the most general level, the common good and human flourishing can occur when just and trusting relationships are developed at both large and small scales. The pandemic is a *global*, even a planetary, problem,[25] and issues of justice and trust have to be faced at this level. Human flourishing entails seeking an internationally just order that respects persons, in their relationships, their local communities, their nations, cultures and traditions. This includes inviting people – especially those most marginalized, such as

Indigenous people and visible minorities – to control how their own data is used. And it does so recognizing that our relationships include those with the earth itself – humans are earthlings in mutual dependence with the earth. Recall that species-depletion may well be directly responsible for creating an environment conducive to zoonotic disease, such as COVID-19.

Human flourishing is not defined by any one feature, such as "health," but by several complementary features that also include freedom from excessive government control and full access to the basic resources required for life – food, shelter and human company. All too often, surveillance is viewed merely in relation to its technical or legal aspects. Given its prominence today, in helping to determine life-chances and choices, it should be assessed and judged in terms of human flourishing, within which data justice seems like a good place to begin.

Data justice is visible in *practices* that take care in how people are made visible, represented and treated. The broad brush-strokes of "authoritarian" or "democratic" polities often serve to polarize opinion rather than grappling with the issues of the kinds of practices being performed. The pandemic offers the chance to rethink the categories within which surveillance is discussed, to expose political prejudice and to confront actual situations with a sense of relational priorities – to restore a focus on surveillance *for* others[26] rather than merely surveillance *of* others. The latter is fostered by a "technology first," rather than "people first," dynamic.

Within such a frame, the deplorable disregard for

the disadvantaged does not have to be deepened by surveillance, as so often occurs. Eric Stoddart proposes an alternative: the "common gaze." This aspires to "surveillance for the common good, with a preferential optic for those who are (digitally) poor."[27]

Yes, I am suggesting that alternative surveillance practices can serve human flourishing. The breakdown of relationships described here has to do with over-reliance on distanced means of determining outcomes – social sorting and automated inequality – based on algorithms that all too often reproduce already existing social cleavages and power structures. In turn, the strategic interests of governments, businesses and policy groups lie behind the pandemic tools such as contact tracing and, indeed, the larger systems of public health data platforms. What they tend to miss is the realities of the ordinary lives of those who are most vulnerable, the "usual suspects" that routinely experience the negative effects of historical forms of disadvantage.

But it would be a mistake to leave things there. As I have stressed, surveillance capitalism is marked by its dependence on popular collaboration with its activities. Willing participants of surveillance give the platforms what they want and enable their success through their propensity to addiction. But those who participate in platforms could also do so from resistant motives; subversive *tactics* over against surveillant *strategies*.[28] The same skepticism and push-back could inform more critical approaches to surveillance in general, including pandemic surveillance. We're all implicated in this surveillance – we could be implicated in reshaping it, too.[29]

Is there any reason why the widespread altruism displayed by millions of ordinary people during the pandemic could not continue? George Monbiot points to many stories around the world of people who volunteered, helped and organized assistance, especially among those worst-hit by the pandemic. In this context, the descriptions of what happened to mitigate pandemic surveillance, in Taiwan and Brazil, make much sense. As Monbiot says, "Power has migrated ... from both the market and state to another place altogether: the commons."[30] Community action grew where many governments and businesses failed.

Human flourishing is a multi-faceted condition, but there are some basic features, again, on which many would agree. One is the need for trust; the other, for justice. Each of these is relational. Trust involves having faith in the other, relying on them to be as good as their word – basic to human bonds. Justice involves ensuring the good of the other – treating the other, basically, as you would wish to be treated. It requires fairness. There are other aspects of human flourishing, but in this pandemic surveillance context these remain as vital contrasts to some of the more questionable aspects of pandemic responses.

The Pale Rider may generate debilitating fear and foster paralyzing pessimism. Or perhaps that equestrian specter prompts us to clutch at straws that supposedly save, such as surveillance calibrated to tech-solutionism, platform profit and political power. The doorway to hope described here offers some alternative life-giving possibilities that could help frame in radical ways our post-pandemic priorities and purposes.

Notes

1 Defining Moments

1 See Amy L. Fairchild, Ronald Bayer and James Colgrove, *Searching Eyes: Privacy, the State and Disease Surveillance in America* (Berkeley: University of California Press, 2007); and https://daily.jstor.org/john-snow-and-the-birth-of-epidemiology. See also Lorna Weir and Eric Mykhalovskiy, *Global Health Vigilance: Creating a World on Alert* (London: Routledge, 2010).

2 David M. Morens, Gregory K. Folkers and Anthony S. Fauci, "What is a pandemic?" *The Journal of Infectious Diseases*, 200 (7) 2009: 1018–21.

3 www.who.int/immunization/monitoring_surveillance/burden/vpd/en.

4 Robert Fahey and Airo Hino, "COVID-19, digital privacy and the social limits on data-focussed public health responses," *International Journal of Information Management*, 55 (December) 2020: www.ncbi.nlm.nih.gov/pmc/articles/PMC7328565.

5 Eun-Young Jeong, "South Korea tracks virus patients' travels – and publishes them online," *The Wall Street Journal*, February 16, 2020.

6 Surveillance capitalism was first described by

161

John Bellamy Foster and Robert W. McChesney in "Surveillance capitalism: Monopoly finance capital, the military-industrial complex and the digital age," *Monthly Review*, 66 (3) 2014: https://monthlyreview. org/2014/07/01/surveillance-capitalism; and Vincent Mosco, *To the Cloud: Big Data in a Turbulent World* (Boulder: Paradigm, 2014); but its best-known analyst is Shoshana Zuboff in *The Age of Surveillance Capitalism* (New York: Public Affairs, 2019).

7 www.vice.com/en/article/bv8ga4/sidewalk-labs-abandons-its-smart-city-in-toronto.

8 Sidney Fussell, "The city of the future is a data-collection machine," *The Atlantic*, November 21, 2018: www. theatlantic.com/technology/archive/2018/11/google-sidewalk-labs/575551.

9 Julia Powles, "Why are we giving away our most sensitive health data to Google?" *The Guardian*, July 5, 2017.

10 Albert Camus, *The Plague* (English trans. of *La Peste*) (Harmondsworth: Penguin, 1960).

11 Laura Spinney, *Pale Rider: The Spanish Flu of 1918 and How it Changed the World* (London: Cape, 2017).

12 Nurhak Polat, "Dijital pandemi gözetimi, beden politikalari ve esitsizlikler" ("Digital pandemic surveillance, body politics and inequalities"), *Feminist Approaches in Culture and Politics*, 41 (Autumn) 2020. The English translation of the quotation is courtesy of the author.

13 David Lyon, *The Culture of Surveillance: Watching as a Way of Life* (Cambridge: Polity, 2018). See also Daniel Trottier, Qian Huang, and Rashid Gabdulkahov, "Covidiots as global acceleration of local surveillance practices," *Surveillance & Society*, 19 (1) 2021: 109–13: https://ojs. library.queensu.ca/index.php/surveillance-and-society/article/view/14546/9538.

14 Ian Hacking, "Making up people," *The London Review of Books*, 28 (16) August 1996: www.lrb.co.uk/the-paper/v28/n16/ian-hacking/making-up-people.

15 The term is from Evgeny Mozorov, *To Save Everything, Click Here* (New York: Public Affairs, 2014).

16 Rob Kitchin, "Civil liberties *or* public health or civil liberties *and* public health? Using surveillance technologies to tackle the spread of COVID 19," *Space and Polity*, 24 (3) 2020: 362–81: www.tandfonline.com/doi/full/10.1080/13562576.2020.1770587. Prominent examples of the "silver bullet" of solutionism for the pandemic are contact tracing apps and vaccines. They do indeed help, but in limited fashion.

17 David Lyon, *Surveillance after September 11* (Cambridge: Polity, 2003).

18 Sumit Ganguly, "India's not as safe as you think it is," *Foreign Policy*, April 26, 2019: https://foreignpolicy.com/2019/04/26/indias-not-as-safe-as-you-think-it-is-mumbai-attacks.

19 Naomi Klein, *The Shock Doctrine: The Rise of Disaster Capitalism* (New York: Picador, 2008).

20 Naomi Klein, "The screen New Deal," *The Intercept*, May 8, 2021: https://theintercept.com/2020/05/08/andrew-cuomo-eric-schmidt-coronavirus-tech-shock-doctrine.

21 See https://news.un.org/en/story/2020/05/1064752.

22 This book answers a call from Martin French and Torin Monahan for research that frames the pandemic as a *social* problem, examining among other things vulnerability and structural inequality in relation to surveillance. See "Dis-ease surveillance: How might Surveillance Studies address COVID-19?" *Surveillance & Society*, 18 (1), 2020: 1–11.

23 Sebastian Klovig Skelton, interview with Shoshana Zuboff: "Surveillance capitalism in the age of COVID-19," *Computer Weekly*, May 13, 2020: www.computerweekly.com/feature/Surveillance-capitalism-in-the-age-of-Covid-19.

24 Achille Mbembe, "Necropolitics," *Public Culture*, 15 (1) 2003: 11–40: https://warwick.ac.uk/fac/arts/english/currentstudents/postgraduate/masters/modules/postcol_theory/mbembe_22necropolitics22.pdf. See also

Namrata Verghese, "What is necropolitics? The political calculation of life and death," *Teen Vogue*, March 10, 2021: www.teenvogue.com/story/what-is-necropolitics.

25 Deborah Lupton, "Digital health and the coronavirus crisis," *Medium*: https://deborahalupton.medium.com/digital-health-and-the-coronavirus-crisis-three-sociological-perspectives-10ec9e01ade4.

26 H. Caren Ates, Ali K. Yetisen, and Can Dincer, "Wearable devices for the detection of COVID-19," *Nature Electronics*, 4 2021: 13–14: www.nature.com/articles/s41928-020-00533-1.

27 David Lyon (ed.), *Surveillance as Social Sorting: Privacy Risk and Digital Discrimination* (London: Routledge, 2003).

2 Disease-Driven Surveillance

1 https://apps.who.int/iris/handle/10665/330376.

2 Megha Mandavia in *Economic Times*, May 11, 2020: https://economictimes.indiatimes.com/news/politics-and-nation/new-plea-in-kerala-hc-against-aarogya-setu-app/articleshow/75676487.cms?from=mdr.

3 Sofia Nazralya, *Human Rights Outlook*, September 2020: www.maplecroft.com/insights/analysis/hro-asia-emerges-as-worlds-surveillance-hotspot.

4 WHO, "Speeding up detection to slow down Ebola," 2019: www.afro.who.int/news/speeding-detection-slow-down-ebola-smartphone-app-game-changer-contact-tracing-hotspots.

5 www.bloomberg.com/news/articles/2020-05-21/big-tech-and-government-s-contact-tracing-systems-have-flaws.

6 See www.bbc.com/news/world-asia-55541001.

7 Colin Bennett and David Lyon, "Data-driven elections: Implications and challenges for democratic societies,"

Internet Policy Review, 8 (4) 2019: https://policyreview. info/data-driven-elections.

8 Martin French, "Woven of war-time fabrics: The globalization of public health surveillance," *Surveillance & Society*, 6 (2) 2009: 101–15: https://ojs.library. queensu.ca/index.php/surveillance-and-society/article/ view/3251/3214.

9 In Canada, social determinants of health are briefly described here: www.canada.ca/en/public-health/services/ health-promotion/population-health/what-determines- health.html.

10 Jill Fisher and Torin Monahan, "The 'biosecuritization' of health-care delivery: Examples of post-9/11 techno- logical imperatives," *Social Science Medicine*, 72 (4) 2011: 545–52: www.ncbi.nlm.nih.gov/pmc/articles/PMC7130 908.

11 See the warning in Marcello Lenca and Effy Vayena, "On the responsible use of digital data to tackle the COVID-19 pandemic," *Nature Medicine*, March 27, 2020 – "Secrecy about data access and use should be avoided. Transparent public communication about data processing for the common good should be pursued": www.nature.com/articles/s41591-020-0832-5.

12 www.nytimes.com/article/coronavirus-timeline.html.

13 Chris Baraniuk, "What the Princess Diamond taught the world abut COVID-19," *British Medical Journal*, 369, April 27, 2020: www.bmj.com/content/369/bmj.m1632.

14 Hariz Barahudin and Lester Wong, "Coronavirus: Singapore develops smartphone app for efficient contact tracing," *Straits Times*, March 20, 2020: www. straitstimes.com/singapore/coronavirus-singapore- develops-smartphone-app-for-efficient-contact-tracing.

15 Paul Mozur, Raymond Zhong and Aaron Krolik, "In Coronavirus fight, China gives citizens a color code, with red flags," *New York Times*, March 1, 2020: www. nytimes.com/2020/03/01/business/china-coronavirus- surveillance.html.

16 See CCLA report, "Keep off the grass: COVID-19 and law enforcement in Canada," June 2020: https://ccla.org/cclanewsite/wp-content/uploads/2020/06/2020-06-24-Stay-Off-the-Grass-COVID19-and-Law-Enforcement-in-Canada1.pdf. See also Katrina Clarke, "Police checking on residents' COVID status shakes public trust, says Hamilton civic rights group," *Hamilton Spectator*, August 20, 2020: www.thespec.com/news/hamilton-region/2020/08/20/police-checking-on-residents-covid-status-shakes-public-trust-says-hamilton-civic-rights-group.html.

17 Teresa Scassa, "Pandemic innovation: The private sector and the development of contact-tracing and exposure notification apps," *Business and Human Rights Journal*, 2021: 1–8: www.cambridge.org/core/journals/business-and-human-rights-journal/article/pandemic-innovation-the-private-sector-and-the-development-of-contacttracing-and-exposure-notification-apps/78A78BE8922FD8512A93C6648B76C2CE.

18 Zygmunt Bauman and David Lyon, *Liquid Surveillance: A Conversation* (Cambridge: Polity, 2013).

19 See David Lyon, *The Electronic Eye* (Cambridge: Polity, 1994); and David Lyon, *Surveillance Studies: An Overview* (Cambridge: Polity, 2007).

20 David Lyon, *The Culture of Surveillance: Watching as a Way of Life* (Cambridge: Polity, 2018).

21 For those not so familiar with the idea that platform companies suck up our data for their profit, watch *The Social Dilemma*, a Netflix documentary, released in 2020.

22 www.nature.com/articles/d41586-020-03518-4.

23 www.brookings.edu/techstream/inaccurate-and-insecure-why-contact-tracing-apps-could-be-a-disaster.

24 Andreas Illmer, "Singapore reveals COVID privacy data available to police," *BBC News*, January 5, 2021: www.bbc.com/news/world-asia-55541001.

25 Andrew Urbaczewski and Young Jin Lee, "Information

technology and the pandemic: A preliminary multinational analysis of the impact of mobile tracing technology on the COVID-19 contagion control," *European Journal of Information Systems*, 29 (4) 2020: 405–14: www-tandfonline-com.proxy.queensu.ca/doi/pdf/10.108 0/0960085X.2020.1802358?needAccess=true.

26 Rob Kitchin, "Civil liberties *or* public health or civil liberties *and* public health? Using surveillance technologies to tackle the spread of COVID-19," *Space and Polity*, 24 (3) 2020: 362–81: www.tandfonline.com/doi/full/10.1080/13562576.2020.1770587.

27 Liza Lin, "China marshals its surveillance powers against coronavirus," *Wall Street Journal*, February 4, 2020: www.wsj.com/articles/china-marshals-the-power-of-its-surveillance-state-in-fight-against-corona-virus-11580831633.

28 www.scmp.com/tech/apps-social/article/3064574/beijing-rolls-out-colour-coded-qr-system-coronavirus-tracking.

29 Fan Liang, "COVID-19 and Health Code: How digital platforms tackle the pandemic in China," *Social Media & Society*, July–September 2020: 1–4: https://journals-sagepub-com.proxy.queensu.ca/doi/pdf/10.1177/2056305120947657.

30 Amnesty International, "Bahrain, Kuwait and Norway contact-tracing apps among most dangerous for privacy": www.amnesty.org/en/latest/news/2020/06/bahrain-kuwait-norway-contact-tracing-apps-danger-for-privacy.

31 Ivan Semeniuk, "Government promotes contact-tracing app against the spread of COVID-19," *The Globe and Mail*, June 18, 2020: www.theglobeandmail.com/canada/article-ontario-to-roll-out-contact-tracing-app.

32 News release, Office of the Privacy Commissioner of Canada, July 31, 2020: www.priv.gc.ca/en/opc-news/news-and-announcements/2020/nr-c_200731.

33 E.g., https://iclmg.ca/covid-alert refers to an agreement by groups including OpenMedia.ca, the International Civil Liberties Monitoring Group, the British Columbia

Civil Liberties Association, the Canadian Internet Policy and Public Interest Clinic, and British Columbia Freedom of Information and Privacy Association, in April 2020.

34 Patrick O'Neill, Tate Ryan-Mosley and Bobbie Johnson, "A flood of coronavirus apps are tracking us. Now it's time to keep track of them," *MIT Technology Review*, May 7, 2020: www.technologyreview.com/2020/05/07/1000961/launchinhmittr-covid-tracker.

35 Mozur et al., "In Coronavirus fight, China gives citizens a color code, with red flags."

36 This familiar point is discussed by me in David Lyon, *Surveillance after September 11* (Cambridge: Polity, 2003).

37 Martin French, Adrian Guta, Marilou Gagnon and others, "Corporate contact tracing as a pandemic response," *Critical Public Health*, October 2020: www-tandfonline-com.proxy.queensu.ca/doi/citedby/10.1080/09581596.2020.1829549?scroll=top&needAccess=true.

38 Frank Pasquale, *The Black Box Society: The Secret Algorithms that Control Money and Information* (Cambridge, MA: Harvard University Press, 2015).

39 As reported by *BBC News* (previewing research to be published in *Nature*), May 13, 2021: www.bbc.com/news/technology-57102664.

40 Seth Schindler, Nicholas Jepson and Wenxing Cui, "COVID-19, China and the future of global development," *Research in Globalization*, 2, December 2020: www.sciencedirect.com/science/article/pii/S2590051X2 0300095.

41 www.nytimes.com/2020/11/15/technology/virus-wear able-tracker-privacy.html.

42 Saskia Popescu and Alexandra Phelan, "Vaccine passports won't get us out of the pandemic," *New York Times*, March 22, 2021: www.nytimes.com/2021/03/22/opinion/covid-vaccine-passport-problem.html.

43 Tariro Mzezma, "Coming soon: The vaccine passport,"

New York Times, February 4, 2021: www.nytimes. com/2021/02/04/travel/coronavirus-vaccine-passports.html.

44 Jobie Budd, Benjamin S. Miller, Erin M. Manning et al., "Digital technologies in the public health response to COVID-19," *Nature Medicine*, August 7, 2020: www. nature.com/articles/s41591-020-1011-4.

45 See chapter 1, note 6, above.

46 Matthew Gould, Indra Joshi and Ming Tang, "The power of data in a pandemic," on the UK.Gov site: https://healthtech.blog.gov.uk/2020/03/28/the-power-of-data-in-a-pandemic.

47 See, e.g., Sarah Brayne, "Big Data surveillance: The case of policing," *American Sociological Review*, 82 (5) 2017: 977–1008: www.asanet.org/sites/default/files/attach/journals/oct17asrfeature.pdf.

48 Michael Steinberger, "Does Palantir see too much?" *New York Times Magazine*, October 21, 2020: www. nytimes.com/interactive/2020/10/21/magazine/palantir-alex-karp.html.

49 Jun Wu, Jian Wang, Stephen Nicholas, Elizabeth Maitland and Qiuyan Fan, "Application of Big Data technology for COVID-19 prevention and control in China: Lessons and Recommendations," *Journal of Internet Medical Research*, 2020: www.jmir.org/2020/10/e21980.

50 https://theconversation.com/contact-tracing-apps-apple-dictating-policies-to-nations-wont-help-its-eu-anti-trust-probe-141304.

51 Teresa Scassa, "Privacy rights should drive our approach to personal data during a pandemic," *Policy Options*, April 9, 2020: https://policyoptions.irpp.org/magazines/april-2020/privacy-rights-should-drive-our-approach-to-using-personal-data-during-pandemic.

52 David Murakami Wood, "The surveillance society: Questions of history, place, culture," *European Journal of Criminology*, 6 (2) 2009: 179–94.

53 Zygmunt Bauman and David Lyon, *Liquid Surveillance: A Conversation* (Cambridge: Polity, 2013).

54 David Murakami Wood, "The global turn to authoritarianism and after," *Surveillance & Society*, 15 (3/4) 2017: 369: https://ojs.library.queensu.ca/index.php/surveillance-and-society/article/view/6835/ed_authority.

55 Michel Foucault, *Discipline and Punish: The Birth of the Prison* (New York: Vintage Books, 1979).

56 "Countries are using apps and data networks to keep tabs on the pandemic," *The Economist*, March 28, 2020.

57 Stuart Eldon, "Plague, Panopticon, Police," *Surveillance & Society*, 1 (3) 2003: 240–53: https://ojs.library.queensu.ca/index.php/surveillance-and-society/article/view/3339.

58 Foucault, *Discipline and Punish*, 196.

3 Domestic Targets

1 Michel Foucault, *Discipline and Punish: The Birth of the Prison* (New York: Vintage Books, 1979), 198.

2 Ibid., 195.

3 Ibid., 195–6.

4 See www.un.org/en/about-us/universal-declaration-of-human-rights.

5 See www.cbc.ca/news/politics/william-amos-liberal-mp-naked-parliament-1.5988128.

6 Sophia Maalsen and Robyn Dowling, "COVID-19 and the accelerating smart home," *Big Data & Society*, 7 (2) 2020.

7 Thorin Klosowski, "How your boss can use your remote-work tools to spy on you," *New York Times* "Wirecutter," February 10, 2021: www.nytimes.com/wirecutter/blog/how-your-boss-can-spy-on-you.

8 Aaron Holmes, "Employees at home are being photographed every five minutes ...," *Business Insider Australia*, March 24, 2020: www.businessinsider.com.

au/work-from-home-sneek-webcam-picture-5-minutes-monitor-video-2020-3.

9   Teresa Scassa, "Pandemic innovation: The private sector and the development of contact-tracing and exposure notification apps," *Business and Human Rights Journal*, 2021: 1–8: www.cambridge.org/core/journals/business-and-human-rights-journal/article/pandemic-innovation-the-private-sector-and-the-development-of-contacttracing-and-exposure-notification-apps/78A78B E8922FD8512A93C6648B76C2CE.

10 See the excellent overview in Kirstie Ball, "Workplace surveillance: an overview," *Labor History*, 51 (1) 2010: 87–106: https://doi.org/10.1080/00236561003654776.

11 Karl Marx, *Capital: Volume 1* (London: Pelican Books, 1979), 549.

12 Chris Matyszczyk, "I looked at all the ways Microsoft Teams tracks users and my head is spinning," ZDNet, January 17, 2021: www.zdnet.com/article/i-looked-at-all-the-ways-microsoft-teams-tracks-users-and-my-head-is-spinning, and https://docs.microsoft.com/en-us/microsoftteams/teams-analytics-and-reports/teams-reporting-reference.

13 Ball, "Workplace surveillance: an overview," 100.

14 Cited in Graeme Lockwood and Vandana Nath, "The monitoring of tele-workers in the UK: Legal and managerial implications," *International Journal of Law and Management*, December 2020: www-emerald-com./insight/content/doi/10.1108/IJLMA-10-2020-0281/full/html.

15 CNBC, May 13, 2020, cited by Ivan Manokha, "COVID-19: Teleworking, surveillance and 24/7 work," *Political Anthropological Research on International Social Sciences*, 1, 2020: 273–87 (282).

16 International Labour Association, *Working from Home: From Invisibility to Decent Work*. ILO, 2021: www.ilo.org/wcmsp5/groups/public/---ed_protect/---protrav/---travail/documents/publication/wcms_765806.pdf.

17 Ifeoma Arjunwa, Kate Crawford, and Jason Schultz, "Limitless worker surveillance," *California Law Review*, 105 (3) 2017: 735–6.
18 Eric Charbonneau and Carey Doberstein, "An empirical assessment of the intrusiveness and reasonableness of emerging work surveillance technologies in the public sector," *Public Administration Review*, 80 (5) 2020: 780–91: https://ocul-qu.primo.exlibrisgroup.com/perma link/01OCUL_QU/sk7he5/cdi_gale_infotracacademic onefile_A636800186.
19 Ibid., 785.
20 Quoted by Alex Hern, "Shirking from home? Staff feel the heat as bosses ramp up remote surveillance," *The Guardian*, September 27, 2020: www.theguardian.com/world/2020/sep/27/shirking-from-home-staff-feel-the-heat-as-bosses-ramp-up-remote-surveillance.
21 Egi Sukiara and Akane Okutsu, "Back to the office? How Japan might work after COVID-19," *Nikkei Asia*, March 19, 2021: https://asia.nikkei.com/Business/Business-Spotlight/Back-to-the-office-How-Japan-might-work-after-COVID-19.
22 Susan Brown, "Employee surveillance software demand increased as workers transitioned to home working," ZNet, November 16, 2020: www.zdnet.com/article/employee-surveillance-software-demand-increased-as-workers-transitioned-to-home-working. 15 April Berthene, "Merchants use stores to tap into same-day delivery," *Digital Commerce 360*, April 5, 2021: www.digitalcommerce360.com/article/coronavirus-impact-online-retail.
23 Baruch Silvermann, "Does working from home save companies money?" Business.com, June 16, 2020: www.business.com/articles/working-from-home-save-money.
24 Rachel Connolly, "The pandemic has taken surveillance of workers to the next level," *The Guardian*, December 14, 2020: www.theguardian.com/commentisfree/2020/dec/14/pandemic-workers-surveillance-monitor-jobs;

Kate Power, "The COVID-19 pandemic has increased the care burden of women and families," *Sustainability: Science, Practice and Policy*, 16 (1) 2020: www.tandfonline.com/doi/full/10.1080/15487733.2020.1776561.

25 This phenomenon also applies to university faculty, where surveillance may be carried out not only by university administrative bodies but also by platforms such as ResearchGate or Academia.edu, dedicated to "networking" between researchers. See, e.g., David Lyon and Lucas Melgaço, "Surveillance and the quantified scholar: A critique of digital academic platforms," in Leonie Mario Tanczer (ed.), "Online Surveillance, Censorship, and Encryption in Academia," special issue of *International Studies Perspectives*, 21 (1) 2019: 1–36.

26 See Maalsen and Dowling, "COVID-19 and the accelerating smart home," 4.

27 Ron Deibert, "Watch what you say," *The Globe and Mail*, November 21, 2020, "Opinion," 3.

28 Katherine Mangan, "The surveilled student," *Chronicle of Higher Education*, February 15, 2021: www.chronicle.com/article/the-surveilled-student?cid=gen_sign_in.

29 Jason Kelley, Bill Budington and Sophia Cope, "Proctoring tools and dragnet investigations rob students of due process," Electronic Frontier Foundation, April 15, 2021: www.eff.org/deeplinks/2021/04/proctoring-tools-and-dragnet-investigations-rob-students-due-process.

30 Colleen Flaherty, "Big Proctor," Inside Higher Ed, May 11, 2020: www.insidehighered.com/news/2020/05/11/online-proctoring-surging-during-covid-19.

31 Margaret Finders and Joaquin Muñoz, "Cameras on: Surveillance in the time of COVID-19," Inside Higher Ed, March 3, 2021: www.insidehighered.com/advice/2021/03/03/why-its-wrong-require-students-keep-their-cameras-online-classes-opinion.

32 Jane Bailey, Jacquelyn Burkell, Priscilla Regan and Valerie Steeves, "Children's privacy is at risk with rapid

shifts to online schooling under coronavirus," The Conversation, April 21, 2020: https://theconversation. com/childrens-privacy-is-at-risk-with-rapid-shifts-to-online-schooling-under-coronavirus-135787.

33 Kate Gibson, "Google secretly monitors millions of schoolkids, lawsuit alleges," *CBS News*, February 21, 2020: www.cbsnews.com/news/google-education-spies-on-collects-data-on-millions-of-kids-alleges-lawsuit-new-mexico-attorney-general.

34 Chuangmei Dong, Simin Cao, and Hui Li, "Young children's online learning during COVID-19 pandemic: Chinese parents' beliefs and attitudes," *Child Youth Services Review*, November 2020: www.ncbi.nlm.nih. gov/pmc/articles/PMC7476883.

35 Sara Morrison, "The year we gave up on privacy," Vox, December 23, 2020: www.vox.com/recode/22 189727/2020-pandemic-ruined-digital-privacy.

36 Sunny Dhillon and Kevin Wu, "Delivery 2.0: How on-demand meal services will become something much bigger," *Fast Company*, February 15, 2021: www. fastcompany.com/90604082/future-of-on-demand-meal-delivery-ghost-kitchens-postmates-doordash-uber-eats.

37 Alnoor Peermohamed, "E-commerce is fast becoming the default option for shopping in India," *The Economic Times*, March 15, 2021: https://economictimes.india times.com/tech/technology/e-commerce-is-fast-becom ing-the-default-option-for-shopping-in-india/articles how/81502440.cms?from=mdr.

38 "COVID-19 has changed online shopping forever, survey shows," UNCTAD, 2021: https://unctad.org/news/covid-19-has-changed-online-shopping-forever-survey-shows.

39 Gabriella Mello, "Brazil e-commerce jumps 57% in first five months of 2020 fueled by COVID-19," Reuters: www. reuters.com/article/brazil-ecommerce-idUSL1N2E02QI.

40 Arjun Kharpal, "China's e-commerce giants get a boost as consumers continue to shift online after coronavirus," CNBC: www.cnbc.com/2020/08/24/china-e-commerce-

boosted-by-shift-to-online-shopping-after-coronavirus.
html.

41 Ryan McMorrow and Nian Liu, "How a pandemic
led the world to start shopping on Alibaba," *Financial
Times*, April 28, 2020: www.ft.com/content/4b1644b1-
aeee-4d02-805a-c3ac26291412.

42 Jay Greene, "Amazon now employs more than 1
million people," *Washington Post*, October 29, 2020:
www.washingtonpost.com/technology/2020/10/29/
amazon-hiring-pandemic-holidays.

43 Emily West, "Amazon: Surveillance as a service,"
Surveillance & Society, 17 (1/2) 2019: 27–33.

44 Leticia Miranda, "With the spike in online shopping comes
a spike in consumer data: What are retailers doing with
it?" *NBC News*, December 8, 2020: www.nbcnews.com/
business/business-news/spike-online-shopping-comes-
spike-consumer-data-what-are-retailers-n1250349.

45 Sonam Sanat, Alessandro Acquisiti, and Linda Babcock,
"Raise the curtains: The effect of awareness about
targeting on consumer attitudes and purchase inten-
tions," Proceedings of the Thirteenth Symposium
on Usable Privacy and Security, July 12–14, 2017:
www.usenix.org/system/files/conference/soups2017/
soups2017-samat-awareness.pdf.

46 Zoom fatigue takes many forms and has to do with the
focus required, especially for our eyes; multi-tasking;
seeing oneself onscreen, constantly; being required to
think in unfamiliar ways to keep up; and being expected
to shift from one event to another with a click rather
than a break.

47 Claudio Celis Bueno, "Pandemia, tecnología y trabajo"
(with English trans. as "Pandemic, technology and
work"), Global Data Justice, December 1, 2020: https://
globaldatajustice.org/covid-19/pandemic-technology-work.

48 Ibid., 196.

4 Data Sees All?

1 Satchit Balsari, Caroline Buckee and Tarun Khanna, "Which COVID-19 data can you trust?" *Harvard Business Review*, May 8, 2020: https://hbr.org/2020/05/which-covid-19-data-can-you-trust.

2 www.axios.com/coronavirus-google-searches-dc47263 3-33c8-4ab2-97db-0f17c8e3d28d.html.

3 Rob Kitchin notes the important but frequently forgotten distinction between a *datum* (that which is given) and a *captum* (that which is taken). When the word "data" is used, people are really referring to "capta" because scientists always select what they need from nature; they never just receive what nature "gives." This misunderstanding causes many problems. See Rob Kitchin, *The Data Revolution* (London: Sage, 2014), 2.

4 Clive Norris and Gary Armstrong, *The Maximum Surveillance Society: The Rise of CCTV* (London: Berg, 1999); Gavin Smith, *Opening the Black Box: The Work of Watching* (London: Routledge, 2014).

5 Such mediation is either what we expect or want to see – the secret agent has been taught what to look for – or technology – CCTV "sees" only what it is directed toward, and "facial recognition" only what the algorithms allow.

6 Margaret Boden, *Artificial Intelligence: A Very Short Introduction* (Oxford University Press, 2018), 1 and 39ff.

7 Michael Roberts, Derrick Driggs and Matthew Thorpe "Common pitfalls and recommendations for using machine learning to detect and prognosticate for COVID-19 using chest radiographs and CT scans," *Nature Machine Learning*, March 15, 2021: www.nature.com/articles/s42256-021-00307-0.

8 This comment, with the one from James Rudd, is from https://scitechdaily.com/300-covid-19-machine-lea

rning-models-have-been-developed-none-is-suitable-for-detecting-or-diagnosing.

9 John Cheney-Lippold, *We Are Data: Algorithms and the Making of our Digital Selves* (New York University Press, 2017).

10 The data-double is discussed in David Lyon, *Surveillance Studies: An Overview* (Cambridge: Polity, 2007), 4–6.

11 José van Dijck, "Datafication, dataism and dataveillance: Big Data between scientific paradigm and ideology," *Surveillance & Society*, 12 (2) 2014: 197–208: https://ojs. library.queensu.ca/index.php/surveillance-and-society/ article/view/datafication.

12 José van Dijck and Donya Alinejad, "Social media and trust in scientific expertise: Debating the COVID-19 pandemic in the Netherlands," *Social Media & Society*, Oct.–Dec. 2020: 1–11: https://journals.sagepub.com/doi/ pdf/10.1177/2056305120981057.

13 Rob Kitchin, "Civil liberties *or* public health or civil liberties *and* public health? Using surveillance technologies to tackle COVID-19," *Space and Polity*, 24 (3) 2020: 362–81: www.tandfonline.com/doi/full/10.1080/ 13562576.2020.1770587.

14 Short Url, "Drones take Italians' temperature and issue fines," *Arab News*, April 10, 2020: www.arabnews.com/ node/1656576/world.

15 Martin French and Eric Mykhalovskiy, "Public health intelligence and the detection of potential pandemics," *Sociology of Health and Illness*, 35 (2) 2013: 174–87: https://onlinelibrary.wiley.com/doi/epdf/10.1111/j.1467-9566.2012.01536.x.

16 See www.who.int/csr/alertresponse/epidemicintelligence/ en.

17 Declan Butler, "Web data predict flu," *Nature*, November 19, 2008: https://onlinelibrary.wiley.com/doi/epdf/10.111 1/j.1467-9566.2012.01536.x.

18 David Lazer, Ryan Kennedy, Gary King and Alessandro Vespignani, "The parable of Google Flu: Traps in Big

Data analysis," *Science*, March 14, 2014: https://science.
sciencemag.org/content/343/6176/1203.full.

19 This section echoes closely Linnet Taylor's work, which
will be carried through the remaining chapters: Linnet
Taylor, "What is data justice? The case for connecting
digital rights and freedoms globally," *Big Data &
Society*, 4 (2) 2017: 1–14: https://journals.sagepub.com/
doi/10.1177/2053951717736335.

20 Aubrey Allegretti and Robert Booth, "COVID-status
certificate scheme could be unlawful discrimination, says
EHRC," *The Guardian*, April 14, 2021: www.theguardian.
com/world/2021/apr/14/covid-status-certificates-may-
cause-unlawful-discrimination-warns-ehrc.

21 Taylor, "What is data justice?" 4.

22 Vino Lucero, "Fast tech to silence dissent; slow tech for
public health crisis," in Linnet Taylor, Gargi Sharma,
Aaron Martin and Shazade Jameson, eds., *Data
Justice and COVID-19: Global Perspectives* (London:
Meatspace Press, 2020), 227.

23 Taylor, "What is data justice?" 5.

24 https://migrationdataportal.org/themes/migration-da
ta-relevant-covid-19-pandemic.

25 Frank Pasquale, *The Black Box Society: The Secret
Algorithms that Control Money and Information*
(Cambridge, MA: Harvard University Press, 2015).

26 Albert Meijer and C. William R. Webster, "The
COVID-19 crisis and the information polity: An overview
of responses and discussions in 21 countries from 6
continents," *Information Polity*, 25, 2020: 243–74.

27 Following Kitchin's observation about "data" and
"capta," data can never be accurately described as
"raw." See also Rita Gitelman, ed., *Raw Data is an
Oxymoron* (Cambridge, MA: MIT Press, 2013).

28 Mirca Madianou, "A second-order disaster? Digital
technologies during the COVID-19 pandemic," *Social
Media & Society*, 6 (3) July–September 2020: 1–5.

29 Ruha Benjamin, *Race after Technology* (Cambridge: Polity, 2019).

30 Stefania Milan, "Techno-solutionism and the standard human in the making of the COVID-19 pandemic," *Big Data & Society*, July–December 2020: 1–7: https://journals. sagepub.com/doi/pdf/10.1177/2053951720966781.

31 Linnet Taylor, "The price of certainty: How the politics of pandemic data demand an ethics of care," *Big Data & Society*, July–December 2020: 1–7: https://journals. sagepub.com/doi/pdf/10.1177/2053951720942539.

32 Norma Möllers, *A Culture of Disengagement: Computer Science and the Question of Justice in Algorithms* (Cambridge, MA: MIT Press, forthcoming), 128.

33 Safiya Noble, *Algorithms of Oppression: How Search Engines Reinforce Racism* (New York University Press, 2018).

34 Katherine Mangan, "The surveilled student," *Chronicle of Higher Education*, February 15, 2021: www.chronicle. com/article/the-surveilled-student.

35 Clare Garvie and Jonathan Frankle, "Facial recognition technology may have a racial bias problem," *The Atlantic*, April 7, 2016: www.theatlantic.com/technology/ archive/2016/04/the-underlying-bias-of-facial-recogni tion-systems/476991.

36 Wim Naudé, "Artificial Intelligence vs COVID-19: Limitations, constraints and pitfalls," *AI & Society*, 35, 2020: 761–5: https://link.springer.com/article/10.1007/ s00146-020-00978-0.

37 Frederick Burkle, David Bradt and Benjamin Ryan, "Global public health database support to population-based management of pandemics and global public health crises Part 1," *Prehospital Disaster Medicine*, October 2020: 1–10: www.ncbi.nlm.nih.gov/pmc/articles/PMC76 53233.

38 Sheryl Spithoff and Tara Kiran, "The dark side of Canada's shift to corporate-driven health-care," *The Globe and Mail*, April 30, 2021: www.theglobeandmail.

com/opinion/article-the-dark-side-of-canadas-shift-to-corporate-driven-health-care.

39 Ian Barns, "On loving our monsters," *Zadok Perspectives*, 149, 2020: 12–14.

5 Disadvantage and the Triage

1 This is the way the situation was reported. Public health workers note that in practice it is hard to tell – as it once was with HIV – who "caught" what from whom.

2 Andrea Huncar, "Black Canadians hit hard by COVID-19, new national study shows," CBC, September 2, 2020: www.cbc.ca/news/canada/edmonton/black-cana dians-covid-19-study-1.5708530.

3 "The impact of COVID-19 on black Canadians," report from the Innovative Research Group, September 2020: https://innovativeresearch.ca/the-impact-of-covid-19-on-black-canadians.

4 On pandemic policing surveillance and social inequality, see, for example, Randy Lippert and Adam Molnar, "Surveillance, police, and quarantining COVID-19 in Canada and Australia," in Claire Hamilton and David Nelken, (eds.), *Research Handbook on Comparative Criminal Justice* (Cheltenham: Edward Elgar, forthcoming).

5 Tereza Handl, Ryoa Chung and Verina Wild, "Pandemic surveillance and racialized subpopulations: Mitigating vulnerabilities in COVID-19 apps," *Bioethical Inquiry*, 17 (4) 2020: 829–34: www.ncbi.nlm.nih.gov/pmc/articles/PMC7445800.

6 "Statement on COVID-19: Ethical considerations from a global perspective," UNESCO, April 2020: https://unesdoc.unesco.org/ark:/48223/pf00037115.

7 Ruha Benjamin, "Black skin, white masks: Racism, vulnerability and refuting black pathology,"

Princeton University: https://aas.princeton.edu/news/black-skin-white-masks-racism-vulnerability-refuting-black-pathology.

8 The term "social sorting" was developed from Oscar Gandy's idea of a "panoptic sort," whereby companies sort customers into categories so they can be treated differently. This is done through database marketing or CRM, and such practices (or their analogues) are now pursued in many other areas as well. Surveillance capitalism thrives on sophisticated forms of social sorting and this fits neatly with the triage approach required for using health data to determine, for example, how testing and vaccine distribution occur. See Gandy, *The Panoptic Sort* (Boulder: Westview, 1993; new edition with afterword, 2021); David Lyon, ed., *Surveillance as Social Sorting: Privacy Risk and Digital Discrimination* (London: Routledge, 2003).

9 See, e.g., Moira Whyton, "Indigenous people don't feel safe accessing healthcare ...," *The Tyee*, July 9, 2020: https://thetyee.ca/News/2020/07/09/Indigenous-People-Accessing-Health-Care-Not-Safe.

10 David Leslie, "Does 'AI' stand for augmenting inequality in the era of COVID-19 healthcare?" *British Medical Journal*, 372 (304) 2021: www.bmj.com/content/372/bmj.n304.

11 Li Yang, "Health Code app needs to be elderly friendly," *Straits Times*, August 22, 2020: www.straitstimes.com/asia/health-code-app-needs-to-be-elderly-friendly-china-daily-columnist.

12 Huizhong Wu, "'Sadness in my heart': Residents of Hubei, China, freed from lockdown, face suspicion," Reuters, April 9, 2020: www.reuters.com/article/us-health-coronavirus-china-hubei-idUSKCN21R1OF.

13 See www.worldometers.info/coronavirus/?utm_campaign=homeAdvegas1.

14 Christopher Parsons, "Contact tracing must not compound historical discrimination," *Policy Options*,

April 30, 2020: https://policyoptions.irpp.org/magazines/
april-2020/contact-tracing-must-not-compound-historical-
discrimination.

15   Linnet Taylor, "The price of certainty: How the politics
of pandemic data demand an ethics of care," *Big Data
& Society*, July–December 2020: 1–7: https://journals.
sagepub.com/doi/pdf/10.1177/2053951720942539.

16   Apoorvanand, "How the coronavirus outbreak in
India was blamed on Muslims," *Al Jazeera*, April 18,
2020: www.aljazeera.com/opinions/2020/4/18/how-the-
coronavirus-outbreak-in-india-was-blamed-on-muslims.

17   Ricardo Fogliato, Alice Xiang and Alex Chouldechova,
"Why PATTERN should not be used: The perils of using
algorithmic risk assessment tools during COVID-19,"
www.partnershiponai.org/why-pattern-should-not-be-
used-the-perils-of-using-algorithmic-risk-assessment-
tools-during-covid-19.

18   Stefania Milan and Emiliano Treré, "The rise of the
data-poor: the COVID-19 pandemic seen from the
margins," *Social Media & Society*, July–September 2020:
1–5: https://journals.sagepub.com/doi/pdf/10.1177/205
6305120948233.

19   Ibid., 2.

20   www.statista.com/statistics/1103965/latin-america-
caribbean-coronavirus-deaths.

21   How COVID-19 is accelerating the use of surveillant
digital identities such as Aadhaar is discussed by Aaron
Martin, "Aadhaar in a box? Legitimizing digital identity
in times of crisis," *Surveillance & Society*, 19 (1)
2021: 104–8: https://ojs.library.queensu.ca/index.php/
surveillance-and-society/article/view/14547/9537.

22   Silvia Masiero, "COVID-19: What does it mean for
digital social protection?" *Big Data & Society*, July–
December 2020: 1–6: https://journals-sagepub-com.
proxy.queensu.ca/doi/pdf/10.1177/2053951720978995.

23   Aman Sharma, "Surge in Aadhaar enrollments ahead of
vaccine rollouts for all," *The Economic Times*, January

21, 2021: https://economictimes.indiatimes.com/news/politics-and-nation/surge-in-aadhaar-enrolments-ahead-of-vax-rollout-for-all/articleshow/80374328.cms?from=mdr.

24 https://internetfreedom.in/sign-on-and-support-close-to-10-organisations-and-158-individuals-who-are-warning-against-aadhaar-based-facial-recognition-for-vaccination.

25 "Wallet biopsies on the millions who lack cover," *The Independent*, September 17, 2011: www.independent.co.uk/life-style/health-and-families/health-news/wallet-biopsies-millions-who-lack-cover-5370483.html.

26 Mirca Madianou, "A second-order disaster? Digital technologies during the COVID-19 pandemic," *Social Media & Society*, 6 (3) July–September 2020: 1–5: https://journals.sagepub.com/doi/pdf/10.1177/2056305120948168.

27 Shoshana Zuboff, *The Age of Surveillance Capitalism* (New York: Public Affairs, 2019).

28 Linnet Taylor, Gargi Sharma, Aaron Martin and Shazade Jameson, eds., *Data Justice and COVID-19: Global Perspectives* (London: Meatspace Press, 2020), 11.

29 See Zuboff, *The Age of Surveillance Capitalism*.

30 Clare Bambra, Ryan Riordan, John Ford and Fiona Matthews, "The COVID-19 pandemic and health inequalities," *Journal of Epidemiology and Community Health*, 74 (11) 2020: https://jech.bmj.com/content/74/11/964.

31 Shehzad Ali, Miqdad Asaria and Saverio Stranges, "COVID-19 and inequality: Are we all in this together?" *Canadian Journal of Public Health*, 111 (3) 415–16: www.ncbi.nlm.nih.gov/pmc/articles/PMC7310590.

32 Sachil Singh, "Collecting race-based data during coronavirus pandemic may fuel dangerous prejudices," The Conversation, May 27, 2020: https://theconversation.com/collecting-race-based-data-during-coronavirus-pandemic-may-fuel-dangerous-prejudices-137284.

33 Maayan Lubell, "Israeli Supreme Court bans unlimited COVID-19 mobile phone tracking,"

Reuters, March 1, 2021: www.reuters.com/article/health-coronavirus-israel-surveillance/israeli-supreme-court-bans-unlimited-covid-19-mobile-phone-tracking-idINKCN2AT25R.

34 Shaul Duke, "Nontargets: Understanding the apathy towards the Israeli security agency's COVID-19 surveillance," *Surveillance & Society*, 19 (1) 2021: 114–29: https://ojs.library.queensu.ca/index.php/surveillance-and-society/article/view/14271.

35 Ahmed Kabel and Robert Phillipson, "Structural violence and hope in catastrophic times: From Camus' *The Plague* to COVID-19," *Race & Class*, 62 (4) 2021: 3–18.

36 Stephanie Russo Carroll, Randall Akee, Pyrou Chung and others, "Indigenous people's data during COVID-19: From external to internal," *Frontiers in Sociology*, Policy Brief, March 21, 2021: www.frontiersin.org/articles/10.3389/fsoc.2021.617895/full.

37 Achille Mbembe, "Necropolitics," *Public Culture*, 15 (1) 2003: 11–40: https://muse.jhu.edu/article/39984.

38 Elizabeth Renieris, "What's really at stake with vaccine passports?" Centre for International Governance Innovation: www.cigionline.org/articles/whats-really-stake-vaccine-passports.

39 David Lyon, *Identifying Citizens: ID Cards as Surveillance* (Cambridge: Polity, 2009), and Ozgün Topak and David Lyon, "Promoting global identification, corporations, IGOs and ID card systems," in Kirstie Ball and Laureen Snider, eds., *The Surveillance-Industrial Complex: A Political Economy of Surveillance* (London and New York: Routledge, 2013), 27–43.

40 See David Child, "A can of worms: Experts weigh in on the vaccine passport debate," *Al Jazeera*, March 14, 2021: www.aljazeera.com/news/2021/3/14/vaccine-passport-qa.

41 Aubrey Allegretti and Robert Booth, "Covid status certificate could be unlawful discrimination, says EHRC,"

The Guardian, April 14, 2021: www.theguardian.com/world/2021/apr/14/covid-status-certificates-may-cause-unlawful-discrimination-warns-ehrc.

42 Joshua Cohen, "Covid-19 vaccine passports could exacerbate global inequities," *Forbes*, March 4, 2021: www.forbes.com/sites/joshuacohen/2021/03/04/vaccine-passports-could-exacerbate-global-inequities/?sh=7ccc367e7874.

43 Stephen Thrasher, "Global vaccine equity is far more important than 'vaccine passports,'" *The Scientific American*, April 7, 2021: www.scientificamerican.com/article/global-vaccine-equity-is-much-more-important-than-vaccine-passports.

44 Linnet Taylor, "What is data justice? The case for connecting digital rights and freedoms globally," *Big Data & Society*, 4 (2) 2017: 1–14: https://journals.sagepub.com/doi/10.1177/2053951717736335.

6 Democracy and Power

1 A useful source of global information on political responses to the pandemic is from Privacy International: https://privacyinternational.org/examples/tracking-global-response-covid-19.

2 Murray Hunter, "Track and trace, trial and error: Assessing South Africa's approaches to privacy in covid-19 digital contact-tracing," The Media Policy and Democracy Project, 2020: www.mediaanddemocracy.com/uploads/1/6/5/7/16577624/track-and-trace-digital_contact-tracing-in-sa-nov-2020.pdf.

3 Naomi Klein, *The Shock Doctrine: The Rise of Disaster Capitalism* (New York: Picador, 2008).

4 "Everything is under control: The state in COVID-19," *The Economist*, March 28, 2020.

5 Ron Amadeo, "Even creepier COVID tracking: Google silently pushed apps to users' phones," Ars Technica,

June 21, 2021: https://arstechnica.com/gadgets/2021/06/
even-creepier-covid-tracking-google-silently-pushed-
app-to-users-phones.

6   www.weforum.org/agenda/2020/02/coronavirus-chines
    e-companies-response.

7   Lily Kuo and Niko Kommenda, "What is China's Belt
    and Road initiative?" *The Guardian*, July 30, 2018:
    www.theguardian.com/cities/ng-interactive/2018/jul/30/
    what-china-belt-road-initiative-silk-road-explainer; and
    www.sciencedirect.com/science/article/pii/S2590051
    X20300095 on China.

8   Dating the arrival of surveillance capitalism is difficult,
    but it is largely a 21st-century phenomenon and did not
    really become fully evident until, say, 2005. SARS broke
    out in 2008 but how far surveillance capitalism was
    relevant to responses is a matter of debate. Whatever the
    case, it was surveillance capitalism *avant la lettre*. It was
    only so-named from about 2008.

9   Arundati Roy, "The pandemic is a portal," *Financial
    Times*, April 3, 2020: www.ft.com/content/10d8f5
    e8-74eb-11ea-95fe-fcd274e920ca.

10 Jatin Anand, "In Delhi, pet crematorium to be used for
    last rites of COVID patients," *The Hindu*, April 30, 2021:
    www.thehindu.com/news/cities/Delhi/pet-cremator
    ium-to-be-used-for-last-rites-of-covid-patients/article344
    44826.ece.

11 "India COVID death toll tops 200,000 as essential
    supplies run out," *Al Jazeera*, April 28, 2021: www.
    aljazeera.com/news/2021/4/28/india-virus-death-toll-
    tops-200000-essential-supplies-run-out.

12 The Chinese government regards Taiwan as part of
    China, and appears to have the ear of the WHO, which
    includes Taiwan's health statistics as subsumed within
    China's. Hence the lack of acknowledgment by the
    WHO of Taiwan's relative success. See www.bbc.com/
    news/world-asia-52088167.

13 Jennifer Summers et al., "Potential lessons from the

Taiwan and New Zealand health responses to the COVID-19 pandemic," *The Lancet*, 4 (October, 2020): 100044: www.thelancet.com/journals/lanwpc/article/ PIIS2666-6065(20)30044-4/fulltext.

14 "Coronavirus: How does the test-and-trace system work?" BBC, March 10, 2020: www.bbc.com/news/ explainers-52442754.

15 Rajeev Syal, "No evidence 22bn Test-and-Trace scheme cut COVID rates in England, say MPs," *The Guardian*, March 10, 2021: www.theguardian.com/world/2021/ mar/10/no-evidence-22bn-test-and-trace-scheme-cut-covid-rates-in-england-say-mps.

16 See www.bbc.com/news/technology-57102664.

17 Gemma Newlands, Christof Lutz and Aurelia Tamó-Larrieux, "Innovation under pressure: Implications for data privacy during COVID-19 pandemic," *Big Data & Society*, July–December, 2020: 1–14: https://journals. sagepub.com/doi/pdf/10.1177/2053951720976680. See also Jordan Frith and Michael Saker, "It is all about location: Smartphones and tracking the spread of COVID-19," *Social Media & Society*, 6 (3) 2020: 1014: https://journals.sagepub.com/doi/full/10.1177/20 56305120948257.

18 Özgün Topak, "The making of a totalitarian surveillance machine: Surveillance in Turkey under AKP rule," *Surveillance & Society*, 15 (3/4) 2017: 535–42 : https:// ojs.library.queensu.ca/index.php/surveillance-and-society/article/view/6614; David Lyon, *Surveillance after September 11* (Cambridge: Polity, 2003).

19 Rob Kitchin, "Civil liberties *or* public health or civil liberties *and* public health? Using surveillance technologies to tackle the spread of COVID-19," *Space and Polity*, 24 (3) 2020: 362–81: www.tandfonline.com/doi/ full/10.1080/13562576.2020.1770587.

20 In Canada, legal requirements for handling data relating to the pandemic were quietly amended in March 2020, in both Ontario and British Columbia (healthcare comes

under provincial jurisdiction in Canada). See, e.g., Sarah Villeneuve and Darren Elias, "Surveillance creep: Data collection and privacy in Canada during COVID-19," Brookfield Institute, September 2, 2020: https://brookfieldinstitute.ca/surveillance-creep-data-collection-and-privacy-in-canada-during-covid-19.

21 David Murakami Wood, "Japan: High and low tech responses," in Linnet Taylor, Gargi Sharma, Aaron Martin and Shazade Jameson, eds., *Data Justice and COVID19: Global Perspectives* (London: Meatspace Press).

22 George Baca, "Eastern surveillance, Western malaise, and South Korea's COVID-19 response: Oligarchic power in Hell Joseon," *Dialectical Anthropology*, 44, 2020: 301–7: https://link-springer-com.proxy.queensu.ca/content/pdf/10.1007/s10624-020-09609-y.pdf.

23 Junghwan Kim and Mei-Po Kwan, "An examination of people's privacy concerns, perceptions of social benefits, and acceptance of COVID-19 mitigations measures that harness location information: A comparative study of the U.S. and South Korea," *International Journal of Geo-Information*, 10 (1) 2021: www.mdpi.com/2220-9964/10/1/25.

24 Craig Timber, Elizabeth Dwoskin and Drew Harwell, "Governments around the world are trying a new weapon against coronavirus: The smartphone," *Washington Post*, April 17, 2020: www.washingtonpost.com/technology/2020/04/17/governments-around-world-are-trying-new-weapon-against-coronavirus-your-smartphone.

25 Katerini Tagmatarchi Storeng and Antoine de Bengy Puyvallée, "The smartphone pandemic: How Big Tech and public health authorities partner in the digital response to covid-19," *Global Public Health*, February 2021: www.tandfonline.com/doi/full/10.1080/17441692.2021.1882530.

26 Shoshana Zuboff, *The Age of Surveillance Capitalism* (New York: Public Affairs, 2019).
27 Jonathan Cinnamon, "Social injustice in surveillance capitalism," *Surveillance & Society*, 15 (5) 2017: 609–25.
28 Rafael Evangelista and Rodrigo Firmino, "Pandemic technopolitics in the Global South," unpublished paper presented at the Surveillance Studies Centre, Queen's University, Canada, in October 2020.
29 Rafael Evangelista and Rodrigo Firmino, "Modes of pandemic existence: Territory, inequality and technology," in Linnet Taylor, Gargi Sharma, Aaron Martin and Shazade Jameson, eds., *Data Justice and COVID-19: Global Perspectives* (London: Meatspace Press, 2020): https://issuu.com/meatspacepress/docs/msp_data_justice_covid-19_digital_issuu.
30 Ron Deibert, "Watch what you say," *The Globe and Mail*, November 21, 2020, "Opinion," 3.
31 Carmel Shachar, Sara Gerke and Eli Adashi, "Pandemics: Ethical implementation imperatives," Hastings Center Report, May–June 2020: https://onlinelibrary-wiley-com.proxy.queensu.ca/doi/pdfdirect/10.1002/hast.1125.
32 Quoted in Maya Wang, "China: Fighting COVID-19 with automated tyranny," *The Diplomat*, April 1, 2020: https://thediplomat.com/2020/03/china-fighting-covid-19-with-automated-tyranny.
33 Jiwei Ci, *Democracy in China: The Coming Crisis* (Cambridge, MA: Harvard University Press, 2019).
34 Azadeh Akbari, "Authoritarian surveillance: A Corona test," *Surveillance & Society*, 19 (1) 2021: 98–103: https://ojs.library.queensu.ca/index.php/surveillance-and-society/article/view/14545/9536.
35 Marcella Casiano, Kevin D. Haggerty and Ausma Bernot, "China's response to the COVID-19 pandemic: Surveillance and autonomy," *Surveillance & Society*, 19 (1) 2021: 94–7: https://ojs.library.queensu.ca/index.php/surveillance-and-society/article/view/14550/9535.

36 Midori Ogasawara, "The rise of pandemic surveillance capitalism: The digital net can incarcerate us without a wall," *Sekai*, 943, April 2021: 96–104 (English trans. courtesy of the author).
37 Civicus Monitor, "Country rating changes," 2020: https://findings2020.monitor.civicus.org/rating-changes. html, reported by Kate Hodal, "COVID used as pretext to curtail civil rights around the world, finds report," *The Guardian*, December 9, 2020: www.theguardian.com/ global-development/2020/dec/09/covid-used-as-pretext-to-curtail-civil-rights-around-the-world-finds-report.
38 Kitchin, "Civil liberties *or* public health?" 9.
39 See Lyon, *Surveillance after September 11*.
40 Kristine Eck and Sophia Hatz, "State surveillance and the COVID-19 crisis," *Journal of Human Rights*, 19 (5) 2020: 603–12: www-tandfonline-com.proxy.queensu. ca/doi/pdf/10.1080/14754835.2020.1816163?needAcce ss=true.
41 Kalindi Kokal and Vidya Subramanian, "Locking down on rights: Surveillance and administrative ambiguity in the pandemic," *Engage: Economic and Political Weekly*, 55 (19) 2020: www.epw.in/engage/article/locking-down-rights-surveillance-and-ambiguity-covid-19.
42 Tim Dare, March 1, 2021: https://theconversation.com/ before-we-introduce-vaccine-passports-we-need-to-know-how-theyll-be-used-156197.
43 Max Fisher, "Vaccine passports: COVID's next political flashpoint," *New York Times*, updated April 26, 2021: www.nytimes.com/2021/03/02/world/europe/passports-covid-vaccine.html.
44 Tariro Mzezewa, "Coming soon: The 'vaccine passport,'" *New York Times*, February 4, 2021: www.nytimes. com/2021/02/04/travel/coronavirus-vaccine-passports. html.
45 Claire Loughnan and Sarah Dehm, "A COVID 'vaccine passport' may further disadvantage refugees and asylum seekers," The Conversation, February 25, 2021:

https://theconversation.com/a-covid-vaccine-passport-may-further-disadvantage-refugees-and-asylum-seekers-155287.

46 See, e.g., Patrick J. Eddington, "Surveillance 'reform': The Fourth Amendment's long, slow goodbye," *Just Security*, October 16, 2017: www.cato.org/commentary/surveillance-reform-fourth-amendments-long-slow-goodbye?queryID=69f02c67cb103a178334b67f09bf4b98.

47 Eck and Hatz, "State surveillance and the COVID-19 crisis," 607.

48 David Gerschgorn, "COVID-19 ushered in a new era of government surveillance: Government mandated drone surveillance and location-tracking apps could be here to stay," *OneZero*, December 28, 2020: https://onezero.medium.com/covid-19-ushered-in-a-new-era-of-government-surveillance-414afb7e4220.

49 Louise Abramowitz, "Israel is using emergency pandemic measures to surveil Palestinian protesters," *Jacobin*, May 19, 2021: https://jacobinmag.com/2021/05/israel-covid-19-pandemic-surveillance-measures-palestine-protest.

50 Smith Oduro-Marfo, "Transient crisis, permanent registries," in Taylor et al., eds., *Data Justice and COVID-19*, 140–5.

51 "Policy and institutional responses to COVID-19: New Zealand," Brookings Doha Center, 2021: www.brookings.edu/wp-content/uploads/2021/01/MENA-COVID-19-Survey-New-Zealand-.pdf.

7 Doorway to Hope

1 See, e.g., Simon Dein, "COVID-19 and the apocalypse: Religious and secular perspectives," *Journal of Religion and Health*, 60 (1) 2021: 5–15: www.ncbi.nlm.nih.gov/pmc/articles/PMC7598223.

2 Such an analysis would indicate that the Apocalypse was

written in the first century, for Christians living precarious lives under Roman imperial rule. "John-the-Elder," its writer, was given a vision of a world-put-to-rights that centers on "rule" of an entirely different kind, in which a renewed environment, justice-and-peace for all, is guaranteed by the "slain lamb" who now lives *among* people from every tribe and nation on earth. As a vision, it exudes both mystery and hope.

3 John Milbank and Adrian Pabst, "How the EU could model a new economic model for a post-pandemic world," *New Statesman*, June 7, 2020: www.newstatesman.com/world/europe/2020/06/EU-economic-model-globalisation-post-covid-trade.

4 Michael J. Selgelid, "Gain-of-function research: Ethical analysis," *Science and Engineering Ethics*, 22, 2016: 923–64: https://link.springer.com/article/10.1007/s11948-016-9810-1.

5 See the parallel discussion in Matthew B. Crawford, "Reclaiming self-rule in the digital dystopia," *American Compass*, June 1, 2021: https://americancompass.org/essays/reclaiming-self-rule-in-the-digital-dystopia.

6 Kelsie Nabben, "Hacking the pandemic: How Taiwan's digital democracy holds the pandemic at bay," The Conversation, September 11, 2020: https://theconversation.com/hacking-the-pandemic-how-taiwans-digital-democracy-holds-covid-19-at-bay-145023.

7 Ibid.

8 Linda Hsieh and John Child, "What coronavirus success of Taiwan and Iceland has in common," The Conversation, June 29, 2020: https://theconversation.com/what-coronavirus-success-of-taiwan-and-iceland-has-in-common-140455.

9 Andrew Leonard, "How Taiwan's unlikely Digital Minister hacked the pandemic," *Wired*, July 23, 2020: www.wired.com/story/how-taiwans-unlikely-digital-minister-hacked-the-pandemic.

10 Rafael Evangelista, "Necropolitics and neoliberalism in

the push for surveillance capitalism in Brazil," in Mizue Aizeki, Matt Mahmoudi and Coline Schupfer (eds.), *Fighting Global Apartheid and Technologies of Violence* (Chicago: Haymarket Books, forthcoming); and Rafael Evangelista and Rodrigo Firmino, "Modes of pandemic existence: Territory, inequality and technology," in Linnet Taylor, Gargi Sharma, Aaron Martin and Shazade Jameson, eds., *Data Justice and COVID-19: Global Perspectives* (London: Meatspace Press, 2020).

11 Details mentioned in this section are from Alcides Eduardo dos Reis Peron, Daniel Edler Duarte, Letícia Simões-Gomes and Marcelo Batista Nery, "Viral surveillance: Governing social isolation in São Paulo, Brazil, during the COVID-19 pandemic," *Social Science & Humanities Open*, 3, 2021: 1–10: www.sciencedirect.com/science/article/pii/S2590291121000243?via%3Dihub.

12 For instance, Byung-Chul Han's fears for an intensified surveillance future – Carmen Sigüenza and Esther Rebollo interview: "Byung-Chul Han: COVID-19 has reduced us to a society of survival," *Euractiv*, May 24, 2020: www.euractiv.com/section/global-europe/interview/byung-chul-han-covid-19-has-reduced-us-to-a-society-of-survival.

13 Linnet Taylor, "The price of certainty: How the politics of pandemic data demand an ethics of care," *Big Data & Society*, July–December 2020: 1–7: https://journals.sagepub.com/doi/full/10.1177/2053951720942539.

14 Jason Kelley, "Governments must commit to transparency during COVID-19 crisis," March 20, 2020: www.eff.org/deeplinks/2020/03/governments-must-commit-transparency-during-covid-19-crisis.

15 See David Lyon, "Surveillance, transparency and trust: Critical challenges from the COVID-19 pandemic," in Lora Anne Viola and Paweł Laidler, eds., *Trust and Transparency in an Age of Surveillance* (London: Routledge, forthcoming).

16 Kirstie Ball et al. 2018. "Institutional trustworthiness

and national security governance: Evidence from six European countries," *Governance*, 32 (1): 103–21.

17 Katherine Hawley, *Trust: A Very Short Introduction* (Oxford University Press, 2012).

18 Laura Martínez, "Contact-tracing and personal data protection face-off in Mexico City," *Slate*: https://slate.com/technology/2020/11/mexico-city-qr-code-contact-tracing-program-coronavirus.html.

19 David Pozen, "Seeing transparency more clearly," *Public Administration Review*, 80 (2) 2019: 326–31.

20 Norma Möllers, *A Culture of Disengagement: Computer Science and the Question of Justice in Algorithms* (Cambridge, MA: MIT Press, forthcoming).

21 Teresa Scassa, "Privacy rights should drive our approach to using personal data during a pandemic," *Policy Options*, April 9, 2020: https://policyoptions.irpp.org/magazines/april-2020/privacy-rights-should-drive-our-approach-to-using-personal-data-during-pandemic.

22 See Naomi Klein, "How big tech plans to profit from the pandemic," *The Guardian*, May 13, 2020: www.theguardian.com/news/2020/may/13/naomi-klein-how-big-tech-plans-to-profit-from-coronavirus-pandemic.

23 Jacques Ellul, *The Technological Society* (New York: Vintage, 1964).

24 Eric Stoddart, *The Common Gaze: Surveillance and the Common Good* (London: SCM Press, 2021).

25 Göran Therborn, "Opus magnum: How the pandemic is changing the world," *Thesis Eleven*, July 6, 2020: https://thesiseleven.com/2020/07/06/opus-magnum-how-the-pandemic-is-changing-the-world. Note that the "global" is part of the problem; seeing the issues as "planetary" connects with the theme of how humans have negatively affected the environment, in the Anthropocene era. See Erle C. Ellis, *Anthropocene: A Very Short Introduction* (Oxford University Press, 2018), 125–7.

26 This is a theme within Stoddart's *The Common Gaze*.

27 The notion of a "preferential optic for the … poor" is

a play on twentieth-century liberation theologies that spoke of a "preferential *option* for the poor."

28 See the work of Michel de Certeau, *The Practice of Everyday Life*, 3rd edition (Berkeley: University of California Press, 2011), discussed in David Lyon, *The Culture of Surveillance: Watching as a Way of Life* (Cambridge: Polity, 2018).

29 Mirco Nanni, Gennady Andrienko and Alessandro Vespignano, "Give more data, awareness and control to individual citizens and they will help COVID-19 containment," *Ethics and Information Technology*, February 2021.

30 George Monbiot, "The horror films got it wrong: This virus has turned us into caring neighbours," *The Guardian*, March 31, 2020: www.theguardian.com/commentisfree/2020/mar/31/virus-neighbours-covid-19.

Index

Index

Index

Index

Index

Index